*Principles and Standards for School Mathematics* **Navigations Series**

# Navigating *through* Problem Solving *and* Reasoning *in* Grade 6

**Denisse R. Thompson**
**Michael T. Battista**
**Sally Mayberry**
**Karol L. Yeatts**
**Judith S. Zawojewski**

**Bonnie H. Litwiller**
*Grades 3–6 Editor*

**Peggy A. House**
*Navigations Series Editor*

NATIONAL COUNCIL OF
TEACHERS OF MATHEMATICS

Copyright © 2009 by
The National Council of Teachers of Mathematics, Inc.
1906 Association Drive, Reston, VA 20191-1502
(703) 620-9840; (800) 235-7566; www.nctm.org

All rights reserved

Library of Congress Cataloging-in-Publication Data

Navigating through problem solving and reasoning in grade 6 / Denisse R. Thompson ... [et al.] ; Bonnie H. Litwiller, grades 3-6 editor ; Peggy A. House, Navigations series editor.
    p. cm.
Includes bibliographical references.
ISBN 978-0-87353-607-3
1. Mathematics--Study and teaching (Middle school)--Activity programs. 2. Sixth grade (Education)--Activity programs. 3. Problem solving in children. 4. Reasoning in children. I. Thompson, Denisse Rubilee, 1954- II. Litwiller, Bonnie H.
QA135.6.N3742 2008
372.7--dc22
                            2008041737

The National Council of Teachers of Mathematics is a public voice of mathematics education, providing vision, leadership, and professional development to support teachers in ensuring equitable mathematics learning of the highest quality for all students.

Permission to photocopy limited material from *Navigating through Problem Solving and Reasoning in Grade 6* is granted for educational purposes. On the CD-ROM, the blackline masters may be downloaded and reproduced for classroom distribution; the applets may be used for instructional purposes in one classroom at a time. For permission to photocopy material or use it electronically for all other purposes, please access www.copyright.com or contact the Copyright Clearance Center, Inc. (CCC), 222 Rosewood Drive, Danvers, MA 01923, 978-750-8400. CCC is a not-for-profit organization that provides licenses and registration for a variety of users. Permission does not automatically extend to any items identified as reprinted by permission of other publishers and copyright holders. Such items must be excluded unless separate permissions are obtained. It will be the responsibility of the user to identify such materials and obtain the permissions.

The publications of the National Council of Teachers of Mathematics present a variety of viewpoints. The views expressed or implied in this publication, unless otherwise noted, should not be interpreted as official positions of the Council.

Printed in the United States of America

# Table of Contents

About This Book .................................................................... vii

Introduction ............................................................................. 1

### Investigations

**Launching Equivalent Numbers** ..................................... 10
  Focus: Reasoning about Number Relationships

**Block Buildings** ................................................................ 18
  Focus: Reasoning about Algebraic Relationships

**Understanding Area Formulas** ....................................... 30
  Focus: Reasoning about Geometric Relationships

**Scale Factors and Measurement Relationships** ........... 43
  Focus: Reasoning about Measurement Relationships

**Fitness Fest** ....................................................................... 54
  Focus: Reasoning about Data Relationships

Looking Back and Looking Ahead .................................... 65

### Appendix

**Blackline Masters and Solutions** .................................... 67
  Finding Triangular Area ................................................... 68
  Design a Spaceship Panel ................................................ 69
  Design a Cargo Bay Panel ................................................ 71
  Block Buildings, Set 1—A Constant Footprint ............... 72
  Block Buildings, Set 2—A Constant Height ................... 74
  Block Buildings, Set 3—Constantly Cubes ..................... 76
  Measuring Shapes ............................................................ 78
  Make a Rectangle from That Parallelogram .................. 80
  Compare That Triangle with That Rectangle ................. 82
  Compare That Trapezoid with That Parallelogram ....... 84
  Scale It Up, Scale It Down ............................................... 86
  Perimeters and Areas of Similar Figures ........................ 87
  Surface Areas and Volumes of Similar Figures .............. 90
  Scale Models .................................................................... 92
  Fun on the Field .............................................................. 95
  Fielding the Facts ............................................................ 96
  Fitness Fest Investigation ............................................... 97
  Seventh-Grade Performance Data ................................. 99

  Solutions for the Blackline Masters ............................. 101

References ............................................................................ 115

## Contents of the CD-ROM

### Introduction

### Table of Standards and Expectations, Process Standards, Pre-K–Grade 12

## Applet
2-D Shape Decomposition Tool

## Blackline Masters and Templates
(All of those listed above plus the following)
Pattern Blocks
- Rhombuses
- Hexagons
- Trapezoids
- Triangles

Isometric Dot Paper
Quarter-Inch Grid Paper
Fitness Fest: Sample Student Work on the Seventh-Grade Data Set

## Readings and Supplemental Materials

Locusts for Lunch: Connecting Mathematics, Science, and Literature
Richard A. Austin, Denisse R. Thompson, and Charlene E. Beckmann
*Mathematics Teaching in the Middle School*

Exploring Proportional Reasoning through Movies and Literature
Charlene E. Beckmann, Denisse R. Thompson, and Richard A. Austin
*Mathematics Teaching in the Middle School*

Making Sense of Slope
Ann R. Crawford and William E. Scott
*Mathematics Teacher*

Building the Concept of Function from Students' Everyday Activities
Susana Davidenko
*Mathematics Teacher*

Strategies for Advancing Children's Mathematical Thinking
Judith Fraivillig
*Teaching Children Mathematics*

Building Students' Sense of Linear Relationships by Stacking Cubes
Diana Underwood Gregg
*Mathematics Teacher*

Mathematical Tasks and Student Cognition: Classroom-Based Factors That Support and Inhibit High-Level Mathematical Thinking and Reasoning
Marjorie Henningsen and Mary Kay Stein
*Journal for Research in Mathematics Education*

Algebra: Real-Life Investigations in a Lab Setting
Leah P. McCoy
*Mathematics Teaching in the Middle School*

Multiple Representations—Using Different Perspectives to Form a Clearer Picture
Cynthia M. Piez and Mary H. Voxman
*Mathematics Teacher*

Selecting and Creating Mathematical Tasks: From Research to Practice
    Margaret Schwan Smith and Mary Kay Stein
    *Mathematics Teaching in the Middle School*

Mathematical Tasks as a Framework for Reflection: From Research to Practice
    Mary Kay Stein and Margaret Schwan Smith
    *Mathematics Teaching in the Middle School*

Functions from Kindergarten through Sixth Grade
    Stephen S. Willoughby
    *Teaching Children Mathematics*

Polishing a Data Task: Seeking Better Assessment
    Judith S. Zawojewski
    *Teaching Children Mathematics*

# About This Book

*Navigating through Problem Solving and Reasoning in Grade 6* is the last of seven grade-level books that present investigations designed to develop students' reasoning methods and problem-solving strategies. The introduction to the book provides an overview of reasoning and problem solving as they might appear in grade 6 as well as a discussion of the role of the teacher in nurturing the development of students' reasoning and problem-solving abilities. Five explorations follow, each situated in a different one of the five content strands identified in *Principles and Standards for School Mathematics* (National Council of Teachers of Mathematics [NCTM] 2000)—number and operations, algebra, geometry, measurement, and data analysis and probability. For the convenience of the teacher, the Standards and expectations for the Process Standards (which include Problem Solving as well as Reasoning and Proof) appear on the inside front cover of the book.

All the explorations are organized in the same way:

- Focus
- Overview
- Goals
- Mathematical Content
- Prior Knowledge or Experience
- Materials
- Classroom Environment
- Investigation
- Assessment
- Reflections
- Connections

Three different icons appear in this book, as shown in the key. One alerts readers to material quoted from *Principles and Standards for School Mathematics*, another points them to supplementary materials on the CD-ROM that accompanies the book, and a third signals the blackline masters and indicates their locations in the appendix.

All the investigations have blackline masters, which are signaled in the text by an icon. These activity pages are identified in the materials lists for the explorations and appear—along with solutions for the problems—in the appendix. You can also print the blackline pages from the accompanying CD-ROM. Another icon signals content on the CD, which also provides an applet for your students to manipulate as well as resources for your professional development.

Margin notes offer suggestions to help you prepare to use the investigations in your classroom. As your students work, take note of the appropriateness of their mathematical vocabularies, the clarity of their explanations, and the complexity of their solutions. Such observations can help you understand their thinking and guide them in developing

**Key to Icons**

Blackline Master

CD-ROM

*Principles and Standards*

Three different icons appear in the book, as shown in the key. One signals the blackline masters and indicates their locations in the appendix, another points readers to supplementary materials on the CD-ROM that accompanies the book, and a third alerts readers to material quoted from *Principles and Standards for School Mathematics*.

Many activities in this book also support core topics identified for emphasis in NCTM's *Curriculum Focal Points for Prekindergarten through Grade 8 Mathematics: A Quest for Coherence* (2006), which specifies by grade level essential content and processes that *Principles and Standards for School Mathematics* discusses in depth by grade band.

their reasoning. Your observations can also assist you in adapting the activities for students with special educational needs.

Although this book emphasizes reasoning and problem solving, it is not intended to be a complete curriculum for developing reasoning methods and problem-solving strategies in sixth grade. We encourage you instead to use it in conjunction with other instructional materials.

The authors gratefully acknowledge the contributions of Caroline F. Borrow and Judy Melillo for their work with Michael T. Battista on Understanding Area Formulas, of Carey Lade for his collaboration with Sally Mayberry on Launching Equivalent Numbers, of Marilyn Riggins and Jim Yeatts for their work with Karol Yeatts on Block Buildings, and of Sandra Richardson, Sandra Paull, and Jon Postma for their collaboration with Judith Zawojewski on Fitness Fest.

**GRADE 6**

# PROBLEM SOLVING *and* REASONING

# Introduction

*Principles and Standards for School Mathematics* (NCTM 2000) states that "problem solving is central to inquiry and application and should be interwoven throughout the mathematics curriculum to provide a context for learning and applying mathematical ideas" (p. 256). Mathematical investigations that challenge students to deal with nonroutine problems and situations should be a regular part of Standards-based instruction in classrooms at all levels.

Just as solving problems can help students make sense of their changing world, so also justifying solutions and communicating the results of mathematical investigations can help middle-grades students develop and expand their reasoning abilities. One goal is for students to develop ways of thinking about mathematics that encourage sense making and reasoning about solutions and strategies. The mathematics classroom is the primary environment in which students have an opportunity to speak and write mathematics. Hence, it is essential that teachers give students opportunities to communicate mathematically by having them make conjectures, test them, discuss and refine them, and ultimately accept or reject them.

The investigations in this book engage students in extended tasks that enable them to look for relationships among concepts in the five content strands—number and operations, algebra, geometry, measurement, and data analysis and probability. Each investigation allows students to focus on one strand in depth. At the same time, the investigations illustrate how a carefully chosen mathematical task can bridge content areas. For example, in the algebra investigation, students collect measures of perimeter, area, and volume, graph them, and investigate them for patterns that they can describe symbolically. The geometry

*"Problem solving is central to inquiry and application and should be interwoven throughout the mathematics curriculum."*
*(NCTM 2000, p. 256)*

1

investigation guides students in composing and decomposing figures to justify area formulas for such common shapes as parallelograms, triangles, and trapezoids. In the measurement investigation, students use the geometric concept of similarity to describe the algebraic relationships among perimeters, areas, and volumes of similar figures.

## Aspects of Problem Solving

Good problems challenge students to develop and apply strategies, serve as a means to introduce new concepts, and offer a context for using skills. Problem solving is not a specific topic to be taught but a process that permeates all mathematics.

What behaviors might a teacher who makes problem solving a focus expect to observe in the classroom? According to *Principles and Standards for School Mathematics*, all students should—

- build new mathematical knowledge through problem solving;
- solve problems that arise in mathematics and in other contexts;
- apply and adapt a variety of appropriate strategies to solve problems; and
- monitor and reflect on the process of mathematical problem solving. (NCTM 2000, p. 402)

As sixth-grade students work through the investigations in this book, they have an opportunity to solve problems, discuss their ideas and conjectures in pairs or small groups, and justify their thinking to the teacher or to one another. Hence, the tasks in these investigations naturally lead to such questions as "Why?" and "How do you know?"

### Students build new mathematical knowledge through problem solving

Students can learn new mathematical concepts and skills through problem solving. A successful problem-centered approach uses interesting problems to motivate students to spend time and energy and be persistent in seeking solutions. Under the guidance of a teacher who encourages them to reason creatively and make connections among ideas, students can discover new mathematical concepts, techniques, and relationships. New ideas often emerge from discussions among students. Teachers should guide such discussions carefully so that students learn the difference between correct mathematical reasoning and incorrect reasoning and between sound problem-solving strategies and unsound ones. The teacher must summarize classroom discussions so that the students are aware of the new knowledge and skills that they have derived from the problem-solving experience.

### Students solve problems that arise in mathematics and in other contexts

The investigations in this book pose problems for students to solve in contexts that are mathematically rich, appeal to sixth graders, and facilitate communication skills.

*"Middle-grades students ... will benefit from frequent opportunities for both independent and collaborative problem-solving experiences. They will engage profitably in complex investigations, perhaps occasionally working for several days on a single problem and its extensions." (NCTM 2000, p. 256)*

- In Launching Equivalent Numbers (focusing on number and operations), teams of students design and determine the cost of building a panel for a new spaceship that they suppose NASA is commissioning.

- In Block Buildings (focusing on algebra), students explore the effects of differences in the dimensions of buildings on the perimeters, areas, and volumes of block structures that they build.

- In Understanding Area Formulas (focusing on geometry), students decompose and recompose or perform transformations on two-dimensional shapes to determine the area formulas for triangles, parallelograms, and trapezoids.

- In Scale Factors and Measurement Relationships (focusing on measurement), students investigate similar figures. One of their goals is to discover how corresponding perimeters, areas, and volumes of similar figures compare and are related to the scale factors for the figures.

- In Fitness Fest (focusing on data analysis), students investigate data from running and jumping events to determine how to assign athletes to teams so that the teams will be competitive.

The problem posed in this last investigation arises from a real-world situation, as do those posed in the first and second investigations. (Launching Equivalent Numbers involves the design of a hypothetical spaceship, and Block Buildings relates to architectural considerations in the design of buildings.) The context for the other two investigations (Understanding Area Formulas and Scale Factors and Measurement Relationships) is more purely mathematical. All the investigations engage students and challenge them to explore mathematics and think about relationships.

## Students apply and adapt a variety of appropriate strategies to solve problems

As students explore problems, they need to consider a variety of strategies to arrive at solutions. In Launching Equivalent Numbers, they use pattern blocks as components of irregular polygons and explore their constructions to determine relationships. In Block Buildings, they use tables, symbols, and graphs to represent the data that they generate and help them describe similarities and differences in discovered patterns. In Understanding Area Formulas, they use handmade or computer-generated drawings to explore problems. In Scale Factors and Measurement Relationships, they use both dot grids and centimeter cubes to represent figures and explore relationships among them. In Fitness Fest, they discover that they can solve the problem by developing various procedures, but they must justify those procedures and explain how they ensure an acceptable result. Varied representations afford students many different ways to explore a problem and enable those with different learning styles to benefit from the problem-solving experience.

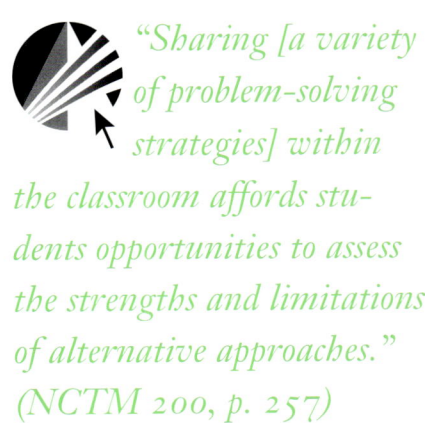

*"Sharing [a variety of problem-solving strategies] within the classroom affords students opportunities to assess the strengths and limitations of alternative approaches." (NCTM 200, p. 257)*

> *"Experiences [in the middle-grades mathematics classroom] should engender in students ... a propensity for reflecting on their work and monitoring their solutions."*
> *(NCTM 2000, p. 258)*

### Students monitor and reflect on the process of mathematical problem solving

As students work through good mathematical tasks, they reflect on their work to determine what strategies are effective and where they need to make adjustments. In Understanding Area Formulas, students conjecture about how to cut a figure to produce pieces that they can rearrange to form another shape, and then they test their ideas by making actual cuts—or virtual ones, with the assistance of a computer applet. In Scale Factors and Measurement Relationships, they explore the relationship between the areas of similar two-dimensional figures, and then they examine the surface areas of similar three-dimensional figures, determining that the relationship that they discovered for area in two dimensions also holds in three dimensions. In Fitness Fest, they develop procedures for composing teams and invite their peers to critique their work, and then they revise their procedures on the basis of other students' comments.

In each of these investigations and others like them, students discover that reflecting on the process used in one problem can help them build a repertoire of problem-solving strategies that they can apply to a wide range of problems.

## Aspects of Reasoning

Reasoning develops over time as teachers facilitate discussions of rich tasks and help students learn "to develop compelling arguments with enough evidence to convince someone who is not part of their own learning community" (NCTM 2000, p. 262). As students reason about mathematics, they should—

- make and investigate mathematical conjectures;
- develop and evaluate mathematical arguments and proofs; and
- select and use various types of reasoning and methods of proof. (NCTM 2000, p. 402)

> *"An important aspect of a problem-solving orientation toward mathematics is making and examining conjectures raised by solving a problem and posing follow-up questions."*
> *(NCTM 2000, p. 261)*

### Students make and investigate mathematical conjectures

Students need to learn that making conjectures on the basis of patterns is a natural part of mathematical thinking and problem solving. The investigations in this book offer many opportunities for students to make conjectures and explain their reasoning about their solutions to problems. In Block Buildings, after they build three sets of five structures according to given rules and determine their perimeters, areas, and volumes, they speculate about the patterns that they observe and test whether these hold for the tenth figure in the sequence. In Understanding Area Formulas, they decompose and recompose figures to see how, starting with the area formula for a rectangle, they can successively determine the area formulas for a parallelogram, a triangle, and a trapezoid. By manipulating the shapes, students investigate why the formulas make sense.

## Students develop and evaluate mathematical arguments and proofs

Sixth graders should understand that solving problems often involves considering examples, looking for unifying properties and relationships, and expressing their observations in mathematical statements that they can evaluate. In Understanding Area Formulas, for example, all students should reason, at least informally, about why their constructions result in a given figure. (Depending on students' previous mathematical experiences, their explanations and justifications will offer different degrees of rigor.) In Fitness Fest, students use a set of data to assign athletes to teams that will be competitive in track and field events. As they begin to develop their methodology, they realize that different events are scored in different ways—high scores are desirable in some events but not in others. Because the students cannot compare the scores directly, they must determine other ways to evaluate the data, such as using rankings rather than raw data values.

## Students select and use various types of reasoning and methods of proof

Throughout the investigations in this book, students have opportunities to justify their reasoning in several ways. In Block Buildings, they discover patterns in data by using graphs to compare linear growth with quadratic or cubic growth. In Understanding Area Formulas, they make conjectures that they then test by using a computer applet or cutting out drawings on paper. In Scale Factors and Measurement Relationships, they use tables and ratios to identify patterns among measures of similar figures. In Fitness Fest, they reflect on their reasoning by applying their method of determining competitive teams to a different data set.

The investigations encourage students to solve problems and reason in the middle-grades mathematics classroom. These processes are important to the development of mathematical power.

*"Students should discuss their reasoning on a regular basis with the teacher and with one another, explaining the basis for their conjectures and the rationale for their mathematical assertions." (NCTM 2000, p. 262)*

# The Role of the Teacher

As students explore the investigations in this book, their teachers should monitor their activities and foster the interactions necessary to maintain high levels of reasoning (see Stein and Smith [1998], on the CD-ROM). The tasks are mathematically rich, but teachers who provide too much assistance or too many clues early in the process can stifle the deep thinking that the work requires. The challenge for teachers is to facilitate communication about a task without directing the students toward a particular solution.

From detailed observations in an elementary school classroom using a Standards-based curriculum, Judith Fraivillig (2001) has identified various strategies that are essential to helping students think deeply about mathematical ideas and share their thinking with others. These approaches, which middle-grades teachers can implement as successfully as elementary school teachers, fall into three broad categories: eliciting

Stein and Smith (1998; available on the CD-ROM) discuss the importance of cultivating habits of reflection on teaching for lifelong professional development.

See Fraivillig (2001; available on the CD-ROM) for classroom strategies that elicit, support, and extend students' thinking.

students' thinking, supporting students' thinking, and extending students' thinking. Figure 1 summarizes descriptions of the strategies in each category.

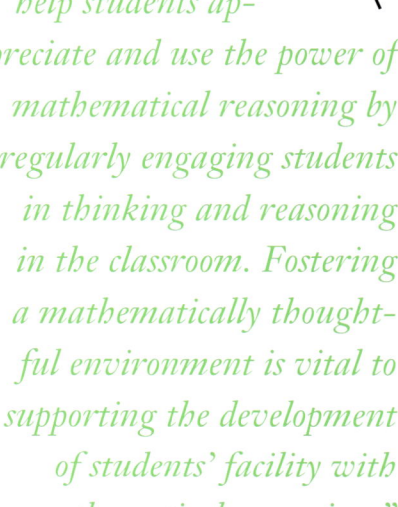

Fig. **1.**
Strategies to advance students' thinking (adapted from Fraivillig [2001, pp. 454–59])

**Strategies to elicit students' thinking**
- Elicit many solution methods for one problem.
- Wait for, and listen to, students' descriptions of solution methods.
- Encourage students to elaborate and discuss.
- Use students' explanations as a basis for the lesson's content.
- Convey an attitude of acceptance of students' errors and efforts.
- Promote collaborative problem solving.

**Strategies to support students' thinking**
- Remind students of conceptually similar problems.
- Provide background knowledge.
- Lead students through "instant replays." (Revisit students' solutions.)
- Write symbolic representations of solutions when appropriate.

**Strategies to extend students' thinking**
- Maintain high standards and expectations for all students.
- Encourage students to make generalizations.
- List all solution methods on the board to promote reflection.
- Push individual students to try alternative solution methods.
- Promote the use of more efficient solution methods.

*"Teachers in the middle grades can help students appreciate and use the power of mathematical reasoning by regularly engaging students in thinking and reasoning in the classroom. Fostering a mathematically thoughtful environment is vital to supporting the development of students' facility with mathematical reasoning."*
*(NCTM 2000, p. 265)*

In addition, research from the Quantitative Understanding Amplifying Student Achievement and Reasoning (QUASAR) Project, conducted in urban schools with underachieving students, found that the following actions by teachers were associated with higher performance by students on a test of problem solving (Henningsen and Stein 1997; Stein, Grover, and Henningsen 1996; Smith and Stein 1998):

- Teachers press for explanations and meaning.
- Teachers have capable students model high-level performance.
- Teachers allow appropriate time for students to explore the task, think, and make sense of mathematics for themselves.
- Teachers note conceptual connections.
- Teachers build on students' prior knowledge.

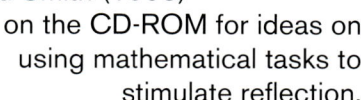

See Henningsen and Stein (1997), Smith and Stein (1998), and Stein and Smith (1998) on the CD-ROM for ideas on using mathematical tasks to stimulate reflection.

Teachers who engage in behaviors like those identified by Fraivillig and the QUASAR researchers can help students develop their reasoning and problem-solving abilities. Teachers can use the following questions to help elicit students' reasoning:

- "Why?"
- "How do you know?"

- "What other problems can you remember that are similar to this one?"
- "What other strategies could you use to solve this problem?"
- "Do you agree with this approach to the problem? Why, or why not?"

Such questions can stimulate important teacher-student discourse that will strengthen the reasoning abilities of all students and can engage students in mathematical communication in the classroom.

The role of the teacher is indispensable, and the investigations in this book are designed to help teachers encourage problem solving and reasoning by middle-grades mathematics students. Engaging students in these processes is an essential component of developing their mathematical power.

GRADE 6

# Problem Solving *and* Reasoning

## Investigations

# Launching Equivalent Numbers

## Focus

Reasoning about number relationships

## Overview

Sixth-grade students can reinforce their awareness of fractional equivalence through investigations with fractional parts that represent the same portion of the whole. They are aware that $\frac{2}{4}$ is equivalent to $\frac{1}{2}$, and they can apply the idea that they can represent a fraction of a unit whole in two or more equivalent forms with different denominators as long as the unit is the same. Students can look for the prime factors of the numerator and denominator of a fraction to simplify it. Giving students opportunities to use and discuss strategies for simplifying fractions allows deep conceptual development.

In this investigation, sixth graders work with equivalent fractions and use nonstandard units of measurement. The use of pattern blocks strengthens an understanding of equivalence and relationships among fractional numbers.

## Goals

- Find the area of an irregular polygon by using an equilateral triangle as a nonstandard unit
- Manipulate equivalent forms of fractional numbers
- Apply the idea that a larger denominator represents a smaller fractional part of the whole than a smaller denominator represents
- Reinforce ideas about relationships among fractions

## Mathematical Content

This investigation promotes the following Number and Operations and Process Standards and expectations for grades 6–8 (NCTM 2000, pp. 393, 402):

*Number and Operations*

- Understand numbers, ways of representing numbers, relationships among numbers, and number systems
- Compute fluently and make reasonable estimates

*Connections*

- Recognize and use connections among mathematical ideas

*Representation*

- Select, apply, and translate among mathematical representations to solve problems

---

*Students in grade 6 should "understand numbers, ways of representing numbers, relationships among numbers, and number systems." They should "work flexibly with fractions, decimals, and percents to solve problems." (NCTM 2000, p. 214)*

In grade 6, students study fractional numbers that are expressed as $\frac{a}{b}$, where $a$ is any whole number and $b$ is any nonzero whole number. Sixth-grade students can build on their understanding of fractional equivalence through the use of various strategies. They can express fractional numbers as equivalent fractions, decimals, and percents. Although students' thinking at this level begins to become abstract, concrete materials continue to be necessary for developing concepts.

## Prior Knowledge or Experience

- Facility with multiplying and dividing whole numbers
- Ability to determine multiples of whole numbers
- Experience in factoring whole numbers
- An understanding of fractions as division
- An understanding of the concept that fractional numbers represent parts of a whole

## Materials

For each student—
- A copy of each of the following activity sheets:
  - "Finding Triangular Area"
  - "Design a Cargo Bay Panel"
- A set of selected pattern blocks, including one hexagon (yellow), one rhombus (blue), one isosceles trapezoid (red), and twenty-five equilateral triangles (green); commercially available or paper facsimiles made from templates on the CD-ROM

For each group of four students—
- A copy of the activity sheet "Design a Spaceship Panel"
- One or two sheets of isometric dot paper
- A calculator

For the teacher—
- An overhead projector
- The following overhead pattern blocks: two hexagons (yellow), two rhombuses (blue), two isosceles trapezoids (red), and ten equilateral triangles (green)

## Classroom Environment

Students complete the investigation in groups of four. Each group designs a panel for a new spaceship that they suppose that NASA is going to build. The teacher assigns the students to various roles—engineer, commander, pilot, and scientist—each with specific duties related to the investigation. Students are responsible for both their own jobs and the group's final product. Throughout the investigation, teachers should encourage discourse among students as they use pattern blocks to determine fractions in lowest terms.

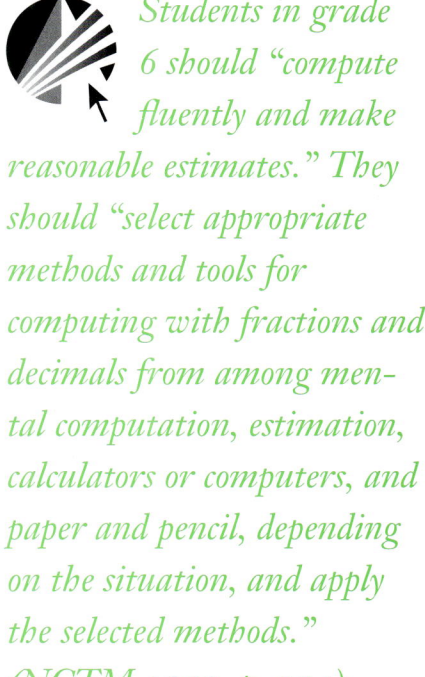

*Students in grade 6 should "compute fluently and make reasonable estimates." They should "select appropriate methods and tools for computing with fractions and decimals from among mental computation, estimation, calculators or computers, and paper and pencil, depending on the situation, and apply the selected methods." (NCTM 2000, p. 214)*

*pp. 68, 69–70, 71*

Paper pattern blocks can be printed from templates on the CD-ROM.

You can use the template "Isometric Dot Paper" on the CD-ROM to print dot paper for your students.

Overhead pattern blocks are commercially available but also can be handmade by copying the templates from the CD-ROM on appropriately colored transparencies and cutting out the shapes.

Launching Equivalent Numbers

## Investigation

Set the stage for the investigation by reading aloud to the whole class the following explanation of the mission:

> NASA is designing a new spaceship. You will be assigned to a team to design the top panel of the new vehicle, which will be in the shape of an irregular polygon. The panel will be constructed of geometric shapes according to certain specifications. The project is at the stage where the NASA engineers are trying to determine the most appropriate configuration of shapes to use. They need to know the total surface area of the panel and what fractional part of the total area is represented by each of the shapes that make up the panel.

Engage the students in a discussion of shapes and fractions. Using commercial overhead pattern blocks or pattern blocks made with colored transparencies, construct an irregular polygon on an overhead projector. Compose your polygon from two equilateral triangles, one hexagon, and one rhombus, as shown in figure 2. Have the students name the polygons that make up your irregular polygon.

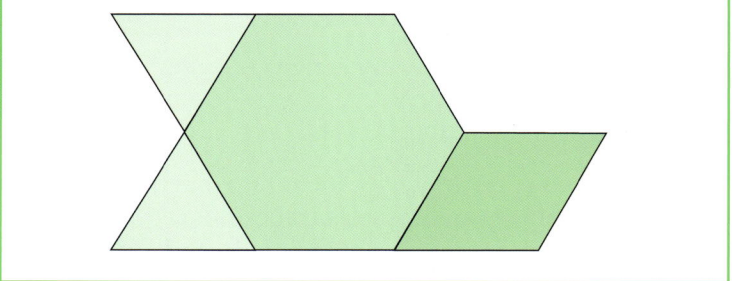

Fig. **2.**
An irregular polygon composed of two equilateral triangles, a hexagon, and a rhombus

Ask the students how they can use a nonstandard unit—the equilateral triangle—to measure the area of the rhombus and the hexagon in your polygon. Let a student demonstrate that two equilateral triangles exactly cover the rhombus, and six triangles exactly cover the hexagon. Explain that the number of equilateral triangles that cover a region can be called the region's *triangular area*. Give each student a copy of the activity sheet "Finding Triangular Area" as well as a set of pattern blocks. Have each student find the area of the figure shown on the sheet in triangular units.

When all the students have finished, explain that they are now doing the kind of thinking that they will do on the mission. Ask the students to describe a standard unit of measurement, and have them give examples. They may suggest inches, pounds, years, square centimeters, or other units. Elicit the information that the larger the unit, the smaller the number of units needed to measure an object. Let the students give examples—for instance, an object whose length measures 60 units in the small unit "inches" measures just 5 units in the larger unit "feet."

Call on a student to display another overhead pattern block—an isosceles trapezoid—along with one of the equilateral triangles and the regular hexagon from your earlier figure. Ask the student which he or she would need more of—triangles or trapezoids—to measure the hexagon. Let other students explain why that they would need only two trapezoids for the measurement, but they would have to have six

A *regular polygon* is a polygon that is equilateral (all the sides are of equal length) and equiangular (all the angles are congruent). An *irregular polygon* is a polygon that does not have all sides equal or all angles equal.

triangles, reinforcing the idea that measuring an object takes fewer repetitions of a larger unit than a smaller unit.

Say, "Now I'm going to assign you to your teams to finish up your preliminary work." Organize the students into groups of four and have them merge their sets of pattern blocks. Then place four triangles, two hexagons, and two rhombuses on the overhead projector in the configuration shown in figure 3. Ask each team to create a different pattern with the same pattern blocks and calculate the triangular area (20 triangular units).

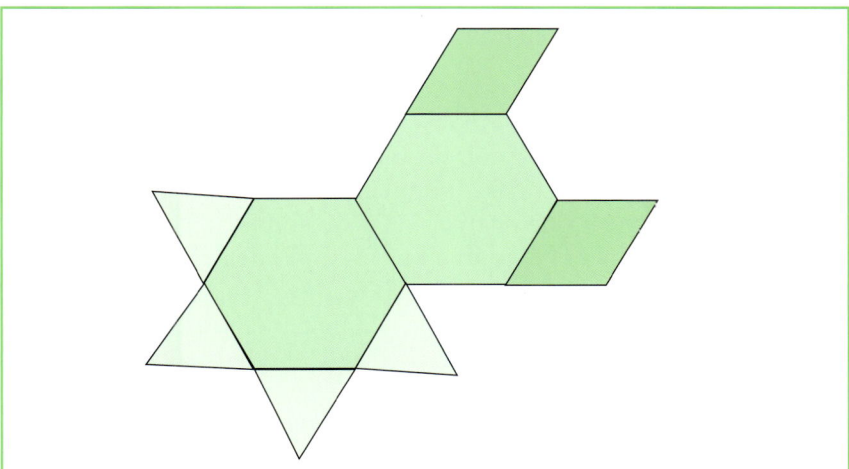

**Fig. 3.**

An irregular polygon composed of four triangles, two hexagons, and two rhombuses

Use the students' calculations of the triangular area to reinforce ideas about the fractional values of the different pattern blocks in various configurations. Again display the configuration in figure 2 on the overhead projector, and measure the triangular area of the configuration (10 triangular units). Ask what fraction of the total area the hexagon represents. Let a student demonstrate again that the hexagon is six triangular units in area and represents $\frac{6}{10}$ of the area of the figure. Ask the following questions:

- "How do we determine the denominator of this fraction?" (The denominator, 10, is the total number of triangular units in the whole figure.)
- "How do we determine the numerator?" (The numerator, 6, is the number of triangular units in the hexagon. The hexagon accounts for, or "takes," 6 out of the 10 triangles in the whole figure.)
- "What fraction of the figure does the hexagon represent?" (Because the area of the hexagon is six triangular units and the area of the whole figure is ten triangular units, the hexagon represents $\frac{6}{10}$ of the area of the whole figure.)
- "What fractional part of the whole figure does the rhombus represent?" (Each rhombus is made up of two triangles, so the rhombus makes up $\frac{2}{10}$ of the whole figure.)
- "What fractional part of the whole figure do the two triangles represent?" (The two triangles occupy the same portion of the

Launching Equivalent Numbers

figure as the rhombus, or $\frac{2}{10}$ of the whole figure, with each triangle occupying $\frac{1}{10}$.)

Point out that the sum of the numerators of the three fractions is 10; that is, 6 + 2 + 2 = 10. Reinforce the idea that 10 represents the total area of the figure in triangles. Demonstrate that adding the three fractions yields $\frac{10}{10}$:

$$\frac{6}{10} + \frac{2}{10} + \frac{2}{10} = \frac{10}{10}.$$

Ask the students what whole number is equivalent to $\frac{10}{10}$. When they give the answer—1—probe further, asking them to explain how they know that this is true. Their responses will vary; one explanation may be that a fraction is like a division problem, and any number (except 0) divided by itself equals 1, so 10 ÷ 10 equals 1.

Next, give each team one or two sheets of isometric dot paper and a copy of the activity sheet "Design a Spaceship Panel." Read aloud the first paragraph, which explains that each team will use pattern blocks to design the top panel of a new spaceship. The panel must be an irregular polygon, use at least one block of each shape, and have a total of at least eight blocks. Also explain that each team member will have a special assignment on the mission—as a flight engineer, a commander, a pilot, or a scientist. Describe each crew member's responsibilities:

- The commander leads the group's discussions, asks the teacher for clarification if the group has a question, and reports to the class on the team's work.
- The flight engineer is responsible for ensuring that the group's panel is an irregular polygon.
- The scientist is responsible for drawing the panel accurately on isometric dot paper.
- The pilot measures the area of the panel, and the area of each component shape, in triangular units.

The team members then determine the fractional portion of the entire panel represented by each type of component shape, and they must show that adding the fractions yields a sum equivalent to 1.

Finally, the activity sheet assigns a value of $450 to each triangular unit in the panel and asks the teams to calculate the costs of construction with their designs. Each team should multiply, using a calculator or paper and pencil.

Once each team has determined the cost of the panel, the commander should use the overhead projector to present to the class the team's proposal, which should include the following:

- The design of the panel
- Proof that the panel meets the requirements of shape, size, and variety of components
- The fractional values of the various components
- The total cost of the design

Have the class identify the team whose design is least expensive and also meets all the requirements.

The students might pursue this activity in language arts class by writing a proposal to NASA. The proposal could take the form of a business letter that would include the information in the proposal as part of an explanation of why the design would be suitable for use on the new space vehicle.

## *Extensions*

Use your students' work to reinforce their general understanding of and vocabulary for discussing fractions. In the panels that the teams designed in the investigation, the fraction of the area occupied by the hexagon is equivalent to the area of two isosceles trapezoids, six equilateral triangles, or three rhombuses. Place a hexagon on the overhead projector, and lay two isosceles trapezoids on it. Ask, "How many trapezoids equal one hexagon?" (two) "What fraction of the hexagon is one trapezoid?" ($\frac{1}{2}$) Ask the students to discuss the relationship between 2 and $\frac{1}{2}$. Do they know that they are *reciprocals* or *multiplicative inverses* of each other? In other words, their product is 1: $2 \times \frac{1}{2} = \frac{2}{2} = 1$.

Next cover each of the trapezoids with three equilateral triangles. Ask, "How many triangles equal one hexagon?" (six) "What fraction of the hexagon is one triangle?" ($\frac{1}{6}$) Point out the 6 and $\frac{1}{6}$ are also reciprocals. Ask, "How many triangles equal one trapezoid?" (three) Let a student demonstrate with the blocks that one-half (represented by the trapezoid) equals three-sixths (represented by three triangles). Ask another student to write the equivalence:

$$\frac{3}{6} = \frac{1}{2}.$$

Elicit the information that $\frac{1}{2}$ is $\frac{3}{6}$ *simplified*, or renamed in *lowest terms*.

Similarly, let students use three rhombuses and two triangles to demonstrate that a rhombus is equal to one-third of the hexagon, that two triangles are equal to two-sixths of the hexagon, and that two triangles are equivalent to one rhombus. Have them write the equivalence

$$\frac{2}{6} = \frac{1}{3},$$

and explain that $\frac{1}{3}$ is $\frac{2}{6}$ renamed in lowest terms.

Remind the students that a fraction is a *quotient*: $\frac{a}{b}$ means *a* divided by *b*, where *b* is not 0. Reinforce the idea that if they multiply both the numerator and the denominator of the fraction $\frac{a}{b}$ by the same number —call it *c*, where $c \neq 0$—the resulting fraction is equivalent to $\frac{a}{b}$:

$$\frac{a \times c}{b \times c} = \frac{a}{b} \times \frac{c}{c} = \frac{a}{b} \times 1 = \frac{a}{b}.$$

In the quotient $\frac{a}{b}$, both the dividend, *a*, and the divisor, *b*, are multiplied by *c*, so the quotient remains the same. Likewise, if both

Launching Equivalent Numbers

the numerator and the denominator are divided by the same nonzero number, the original and the resulting fractions are equivalent.

Also remind the students that a prime number is a whole number that has exactly two distinct factors, itself and 1. Explain that the *prime factorization* of a number expresses the number as the product of prime numbers. For instance, the prime factorization of 15 is $3 \times 5$. Show the students the prime factorization of the numerator and denominator of the fraction $\frac{3}{6}$:

$$\frac{1 \times 3}{1 \times 2 \times 3}.$$

The students can divide the numerator and the denominator by 3, yielding

$$\frac{1}{1 \times 2}.$$

Ask, "What number can you use to divide the numerator and denominator of $\frac{2}{6}$ to get $\frac{1}{3}$?" Write the following fractions on the board or overhead projector, and ask the students to rename them:

$$\frac{4}{8}, \frac{2}{4}, \frac{3}{6}, \frac{5}{10}, \frac{4}{12}, \frac{2}{10}, \frac{2}{5}, \frac{6}{8}.$$

For each example, have the students say what divisor they used to rename the fraction. They should notice that they cannot rename $\frac{2}{5}$ in any simpler terms and therefore must conclude that it is already in simplest terms.

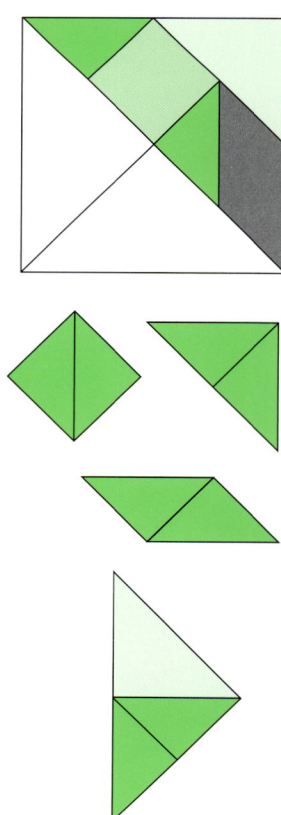

The familiar tangram square (see the margin) offers another, similar context in which to extend your students' work with equivalent fractions. You can ask the students to stack the seven pieces in order of decreasing area. They will quickly see that they should stack the two large triangles first and the two small triangles last, but in what order should they stack the square, the parallelogram, and the medium-sized triangle? Let them discover that they can exactly cover each of these shapes by the two small triangles, so all three pieces have the same area and can be stacked in any order.

The students can also determine the fractional part of the original tangram square that each of the seven pieces represents. Each large triangle is obviously one-quarter of the area, and the students can easily discover that the medium-sized triangle is one-half the area of a large triangle, and each small triangle is one-half the area of the medium triangle. The fractional part of the total tangram square represented by each piece is shown in the margin at the top of the next page.

Let your students investigate other ratios and equivalences in the tangram square:

- If the square piece represents one unit of area, what are the areas of the other six pieces? What is the area of the total tangram square?
- If a large triangle represents one unit of area, what are the areas of the other six pieces? What is the area of the total tangram square?

- If a large triangle represents four (or seven, ten, or another number) units of area, what are the areas of the other six pieces? What is the area of the total tangram square?

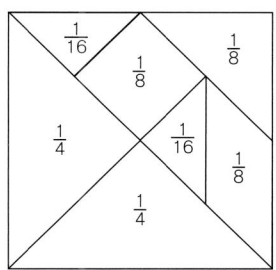

## Assessment

To assess students' understanding of triangular area and fractional numbers and to evaluate their ability to demonstrate that fractions of the form $\frac{a}{a}$ ($a \neq 0$) are equivalent to the whole, or 1, give each student a copy of the activity sheet "Design a Cargo Bay Panel" to complete independently. The students should be able to express in words the idea that when the numerator and denominator of a fraction are the same, the fraction is equivalent to the number 1. They should be able to demonstrate the equivalence by drawing a number line or by expressing such a fraction as a division problem.

Students can see that
$$\frac{2}{4} = \frac{3}{6} = \frac{1}{2}$$
because the fractions are the same distance from 0 on the number line.

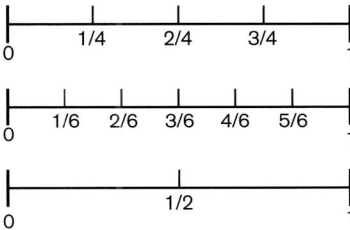

## Reflections

In this investigation, students use manipulatives to help them see the connection between fractional numbers and whole numbers. The context of the investigation—designing a panel for a spaceship—increases their awareness of real-world applications of mathematics. Moreover, working in teams, with each member having an assigned responsibility, helps the students develop a sense of collaboration and cooperation as they discuss, debate, and solve problems together, in the process teaching and learning from one another.

## Connections

Throughout the investigation, students are deepening their concept of fractional numbers. Connections to geometry are evident as they use concrete models of both regular and irregular polygons to design a panel in the shape of an irregular polygon. As they build their panels and calculate the area, they compare fractional numbers. Doing so strengthens a foundation for more abstract mathematical reasoning as students continue to investigate fractional numbers and their sizes.

This investigation allows students to reinforce their conceptual understanding of area, measurement, fractional numbers, and equivalence. Students enrich their understanding by using a nonstandard triangular unit of measurement to calculate the area of irregular polygons, by representing the parts of a figure as fractions, and by simplifying fractions and determining fractions that are equivalent to 1.

# Block Buildings

## Focus

Reasoning about algebraic relationships

## Overview

*Students should be able to investigate patterns and generalize their observations.*

In the intermediate grades, students gain experience in representing patterns verbally, numerically, graphically, and symbolically. They begin to look for relationships in numerical and geometric patterns and analyze how patterns grow and change. Students in the middle grades continue to explore and explain patterns by using tables, charts, graphs, physical objects, words, or mathematical symbols. Sixth-grade students should be able to relate and compare different representations of a relationship. As students at this level continue to explore patterns, their work usually emphasizes those that exhibit linear relationships—that is, those that exhibit a constant rate of change.

In this investigation, students construct buildings from centimeter cubes and explore the effect that a change in one or more dimensions of a building can have on its perimeter, surface area, and volume. This investigation gives sixth-grade students an opportunity to discover how patterns change and to distinguish linear from nonlinear patterns. Although the emphasis is on discovering linear relationships, the students also explore nonlinear relationships and use their models to develop and test conjectures. They compare linear and nonlinear growth by using models, tables, graphs, and algebraic expressions. They learn to relate symbolic, tabular, and graphical representations, and they lay the foundation for developing an understanding of the significance of slope.

*By starting with the concrete representations of the structures, students can understand important abstract concepts, such as functions, and can move with relative ease to the standard representation of the function.*

## Goals

- Use tables to organize information
- Make graphs, using correct labels and scales, to display data
- Recognize when a constant rate of change is evident in a pattern established by data
- Recognize the concept of linearity in real-world contexts
- Identify relationships among tabular, graphical, and symbolic representations of a function

## Mathematical Content

This investigation promotes the following Algebra and Process Standards and expectations for grades 6–8 (NCTM 2000, pp. 395, 402):

*Algebra*

- Understand patterns, relations, and functions
  - Represent, analyze, and generalize a variety of patterns with tables, graphs, words, and, when possible, symbolic rules

- Relate and compare different forms of representation for a relationship
- Identify functions as linear or nonlinear and contrast their properties from tables, graphs, or equations
* Represent and analyze mathematical situations and structures using algebraic symbols
  - Explore relationships between symbolic expressions and graphs of lines, paying particular attention to the meaning of intercept and slope
  - Use symbolic algebra to represent situations and to solve problems, especially those that involve linear relationships

## Problem Solving

* Solve problems that arise in mathematics and in other contexts

## Reasoning and Proof

* Make and investigate mathematical conjectures

## Communication

* Organize and consolidate … mathematical thinking through communication

## Connections

* Recognize and use connections among mathematical ideas

## Representation

* Create and use representations to organize, record, and communicate mathematical ideas
* Use representations to model and interpret physical, social, and mathematical phenomena

## Prior Knowledge or Experience

* Experience in examining data to determine patterns
* Experience in constructing tables from data
* Experience in plotting points on a graph
* Conceptual understanding of the surface area and the volume of a solid figure

## Materials

For each pair or small group of three or four students—
* A copy of each of the following activity sheets:
  - "Block Buildings, Set 1—A Constant Footprint"

Using concrete representations can help students conceptualize both linear and nonlinear relationships.

*Students in the middle grades should be able to "make and investigate mathematical conjectures" (NCTM 2000, p. 402). Teachers need to provide tasks that enable students to explore mathematical concepts and develop conjectures based on their investigations.*

*pp. 72–73, 74–75, 76–77*

- "Block Buildings, Set 2—A Constant Height"
- "Block Buildings, Set 3—Constantly Cubes"
* Three or four sheets of quarter-inch grid paper (template on the CD-ROM)
* 225 centimeter cubes
* A ruler
* Three colored pencils in different colors
* A graphing calculator (optional)
* Spreadsheet software (optional)
* Access to a computer (optional)

For the teacher—

* Enlarged copies of the tables in the activity sheets for classroom display or enlarged transparency copies of the completed tables (see fig. 9) to display on an overhead projector
* Enlarged copies of the graphs in figure 10 for classroom display or enlarged transparency copies to display on an overhead projector

## Classroom Environment

Students may work in pairs or small groups of three or four. After all the students have completed the steps on each activity sheet, they should engage in a whole-class discussion of their work.

## Investigation

This three-part investigation explores the effects of changes that students make to block buildings that they have constructed with centimeter cubes. They build a set of block structures and determine the perimeter, the surface area, and the volume of each building.

Before beginning the investigation, explain to the students that an architect must take many issues into consideration in designing a building. For instance, if a client wishes to increase the height of an office building, other measurements will also change. Ask the students what these measurements are. Elicit the idea that a change in height will result in a greater surface area, necessitating more bricks or concrete, for instance, in the construction. A change in height will also produce a greater volume, allowing for more or larger offices in the building.

Tell the students that they will explore changes in three measurements in block buildings that they construct with centimeter cubes. Explain how they will determine the three measurements in the investigation. The *perimeter* of each building will be the sum of all the lengths of the external edges. A one-block building has twelve edges, all of unit length 1, so its perimeter is twelve units (see fig. 4). A two-block building also has twelve edges, but all the edges that are formed by two blocks are two units long, so the perimeter is

$$1 + 1 + 1 + 1 + 2 + 2 + 2 + 2 + 1 + 1 + 1 + 1,$$

or 16, units (see fig. 5). Point out that in the building made with two cubes, the edges that touch are not edges of the two-block structure.

---

As they construct their block structures, the students might benefit from exploring volume by filling boxes with cubes on screen at NCTM's Illuminations Web site: http://illuminations.nctm.org/ActivityDetail.aspx?ID=6.

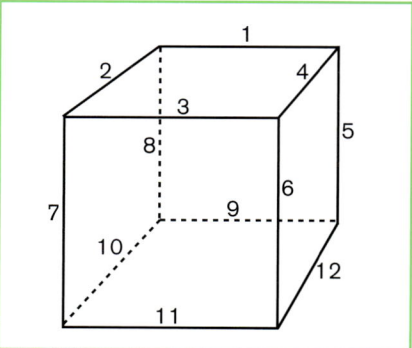

Fig. **4.**
A one-cube block building has the twelve numbered edges, each with a length of one unit, so the perimeter is twelve units.

Instead, they are part of the faces of the prism that are formed by stacking the cubes.

In the investigation, the *surface area* of a structure will be the sum of the areas of the six faces of the structure. Call students' attention to the fact that the surface area includes the area of the face of the building that touches the "ground." For example, a one-cube building has a surface area of six square units—one square unit for each face. In a building constructed from two stacked cubes, the area of the top face is one square unit, and so is the area of the bottom face. Each of the side, or lateral, faces has an area of two square units, so the surface area of a two-cube building is 1 + 1 + 2 + 2 + 2 + 2, or 10, square units.

A building's *volume* will be the number of cubes, both those that are visible and those that are in the interior but are not visible, in its construction. For example, the volume of a one-cube building is one cubic unit. A two-cube building has a volume of two cubic units.

## Constructing and Measuring the Block Buildings

Arrange the students in pairs or small groups to work together. Give a copy of the activity sheet "Block Buildings, Set 1—A Constant Footprint" to each pair or group. Have the students use centimeter cubes to build a set of five block buildings as directed in step 1. The first building consists of one cube; the students form the other four buildings in the set by stacking an additional cube on top of a structure like the previous one. This process limits the *footprint* of all the buildings in the set to one square unit. A building's footprint is the surface area of its bottom face. Figure 6 shows the first set of buildings. When the students have constructed the buildings in this set, have them complete step 2, in which they determine the perimeter, surface area, and volume of each building and record the measurements in the table supplied on the activity sheet.

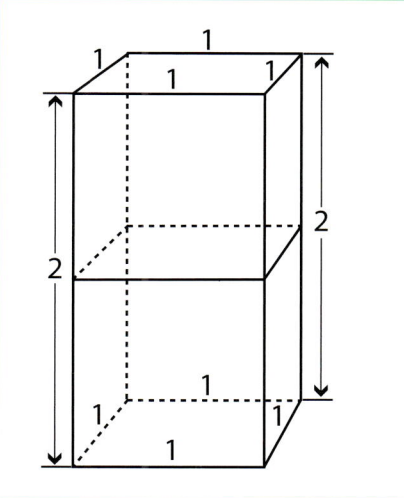

Fig. 5.

A two-cube block building also has twelve edges; four of the edges are two units long, so the perimeter is sixteen units.

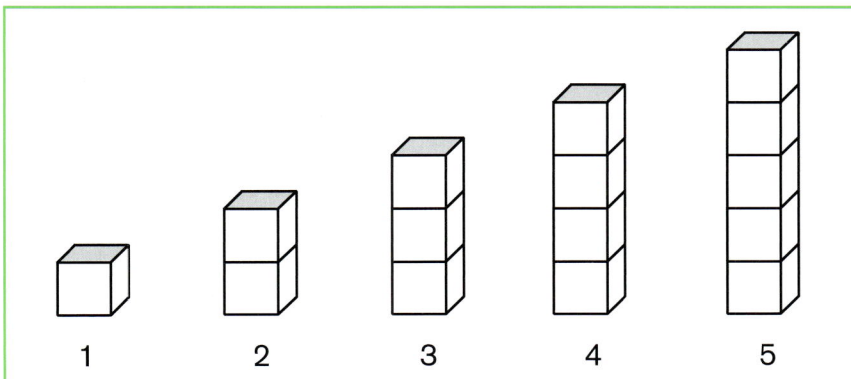

Fig. 6.

In the first set of buildings, the footprint is held constant at one square unit.

The students might also enjoy creating their block structures with the Isometric Drawing Tool at NCTM's Illuminations Web site: http://illuminations .nctm.org/ActivityDetail .aspx?ID=125.

After the students have completed steps 1 and 2 for the first set of buildings, ask them to pause in their work. Give each pair or group a copy of the second activity sheet, "Block Buildings, Set 2—A Constant Height," and direct the students to construct the second set of buildings as specified in step 1. These structures have a fixed height of three units, but their footprints increase as the squares of the consecutive numbers 1–5. Figure 7 illustrates the second set of buildings. Let the students determine the perimeter, surface area, and volume of each building and record the measurements in the table, as step 2 requests, and then ask them to pause again.

**Fig. 7.**

In the second set of buildings, the heights of the buildings remain constant, but the footprints increase as the squares of the consecutive numbers 1–5.

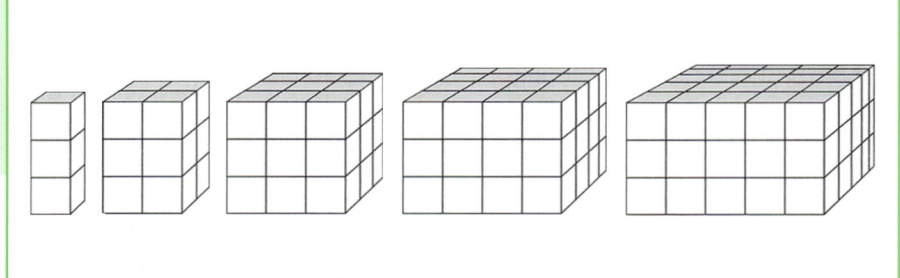

Give each pair or group a copy of the third activity sheet, "Block Buildings, Set 3—Constantly Cubes." Ask the students to follow the same process as before, completing steps 1 and 2, in which they construct the third set of block buildings and determine and record the perimeter, surface area, and volume of each structure. Figure 8 illustrates the third set of block buildings, consisting of successively larger cubes.

**Fig. 8.**

The third set of buildings consists of successively larger cubes.

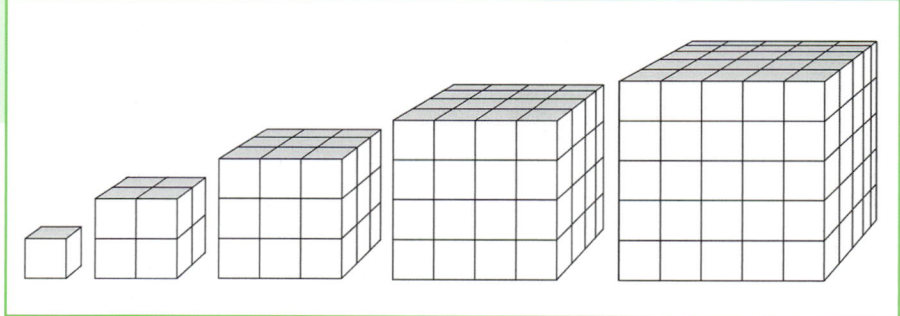

### Determining Functional Relationships between the Buildings and Their Measurements

When the groups have finished gathering and recording the data, direct them to share their results with the rest of the class. Help the class reach a consensus on the measurements for the perimeter, the surface area, and the volume of each building in the three sets. The completed tables appear in figure 9. Use the discussion to reveal any remaining misunderstandings, and take time to clarify how to arrive at the various measurements.

Next, have the students move on to step 3 on each activity sheet. In this step, they discuss the relationships between the number of each building in a set and its perimeter, surface area, and volume. They must describe each relationship in writing, and, if possible, express it symbolically, using $n$ to stand for the number of a building. For example, they might write that the perimeter of a building in set 1 is "increasing by four linear units with each successive building." Or they might express the perimeter of building $n$ symbolically, as $4n + 8$, or $4(n + 2)$, linear units.

The students' responses in step 3 will, of course, reflect their previous knowledge. Only very advanced students will be able to fill in every cell in the last column, under $n$, in each table (see fig. 9). Writing all of these symbolic expressions, or formulas, or function rules, is challenging. Ask the groups to share their rules and explain how they arrived at them. Direct them to test their conjectures and either accept or reject them so that they can eventually agree on appropriate expressions.

See Willoughby (1997) for further insights into students' development and understanding of functions.

Fig. 9.
The completed tables of the measurements of the buildings in block sets 1–3

| | Block Buildings, Set 1 | | | | | |
|---|---|---|---|---|---|---|
| | Number of the Block Building | | | | | |
| | 1 | 2 | 3 | 4 | 5 | n |
| Perimeter (linear units) | 12 | 16 | 20 | 24 | 28 | $4n + 8$, or $4(n + 2)$ |
| Surface area (square units) | 6 | 10 | 14 | 18 | 22 | $4n + 2$, or $2(2n + 1)$ |
| Volume (cubic units) | 1 | 2 | 3 | 4 | 5 | $n$ |

| | Block Buildings, Set 2 | | | | | |
|---|---|---|---|---|---|---|
| | Number of the Block Building | | | | | |
| | 1 | 2 | 3 | 4 | 5 | n |
| Perimeter (linear units) | 20 | 28 | 36 | 44 | 52 | $8n + 12$, or $4(2n + 3)$ |
| Surface area (square units) | 14 | 32 | 54 | 80 | 110 | $2n^2 + 12n$, or $2n(n + 6)$ |
| Volume (cubic units) | 3 | 12 | 27 | 48 | 75 | $3n^2$ |

| | Block Buildings, Set 3 | | | | | |
|---|---|---|---|---|---|---|
| | Number of the Block Building | | | | | |
| | 1 | 2 | 3 | 4 | 5 | n |
| Perimeter (linear units) | 12 | 24 | 36 | 48 | 60 | $12n$ |
| Surface area (square units) | 6 | 24 | 54 | 96 | 150 | $6n^2$ |
| Volume (cubic units) | 1 | 8 | 27 | 64 | 125 | $n^3$ |

Let the students test the rules that they have established by making drawings or paper-and-pencil calculations to find the perimeters, surface areas, and volumes of the next three buildings in each set. They can then compare their measurements with the results given by the rules that they have determined. Challenge them to predict the number of cubes that they would need to construct the tenth building in each of the three sets. (Remind them that the number of cubes is equal to the volume in each case.) Ask what they think the perimeter and the surface area would be in each case.

*Graphing the Measurements*

Step 4 on each activity sheet follows up on the work of determining the relationships between the number of a building and its perimeter,

*Graphs often have a more vivid visual impact than tables do.*

Electronic spreadsheets can help students understand the correspondence between tables and graphs of functions. Davidenko (1997; available on the CD-ROM) offers real-life ideas for using spreadsheets to extend students' thinking.

It is important that the students understand that although the shapes of the three graphs can be compared usefully on a single grid, the data cannot be compared because they represent measurements reported in different units.

McCoy (1997; available on the CD-ROM) offers sample laboratory activities for modeling linear and nonlinear relationships.

surface area, and volume by asking the students to make predictions about graphs of these relationships. What would a graph look like in the case of each measurement for each set of buildings? Ask the students to record their predictions on each of the three worksheets. Give the groups an opportunity to share their predictions and explain their thinking.

You can discuss linear and nonlinear graphs at this time, or you can wait until the students have created their graphs. If you decide to discuss linearity first, explain that patterns in which each new term adds a fixed number to the previous term are examples of linear relationships. You may find it helpful to have either graphing calculators or spreadsheet software available for your students' use. Both technologies are excellent tools for exploring linearity. Understanding that linearity is associated with a constant rate of change between two variables prepares students to encounter the concept of slope in their later study of mathematics. A linear function has the form $y = mx + b$, where $m$ is the slope, or rate of change between the two variables, and the point $(0, b)$ is the $y$-intercept.

After the students have predicted the shapes of the graphs, give three or four sheets of grid paper to each group and guide the students in completing step 5 on each activity sheet. For each set of buildings, they must graph each group of measurements (perimeter, surface area, and volume) against the numbers of the buildings. Explain to the students how to set up a coordinate grid, and help them label the origin and the $x$- and $y$-axes and make appropriate scales.

Step 6 presents a different graphing task. For each set of buildings, the students must now make a compact, composite picture of the measurements by showing all three measurements on one graph. Doing this requires an unorthodox step—one that you should emphasize is not, strictly speaking, permissible on a coordinate graph. The values on the $y$-axis of each composite graph will show measurements in three different types of units—linear units, square units, and cubic units—simply as numbers of units in the buildings' perimeters, surface areas, and volumes. Thus, the $y$-axes in the three coordinate graphs in figure 10 are labeled simply "Number of Units in a Measurement," though in fact perimeter, surface area, and volume are all measured in different units. (As in the individual graphs, the $x$-axes should show "Building Number" for the buildings in the set.) Have the students use pencils in three colors—one color for the data relating to perimeter, a second color for the data relating to area, and a third color for the data relating to volume.

Display on the board or an overhead projector the three tables in figure 9 (also in the "Solutions" section). If you have not already done so, discuss linear and nonlinear relationships. Ask the students which data show constant rates of change and which show varying ones. Help the students identify the data patterns as either linear or nonlinear.

To probe linear and nonlinear relationships, also display on the board or an overhead projector the graphs in figure 10 (also in the "Solutions" section). Call the students' attention to the shapes of the graphs. Linear change can be seen as a constant vertical change between successive data points. The students should note that the graphs of all three measurements (perimeter, surface area, and volume) in set 1 show linear relationships, as do the graphs of the perimeter data for sets 2 and 3. The students may conjecture that the two nonlinear graphs for set 3

Navigating through Problem Solving and Reasoning in Grade 6

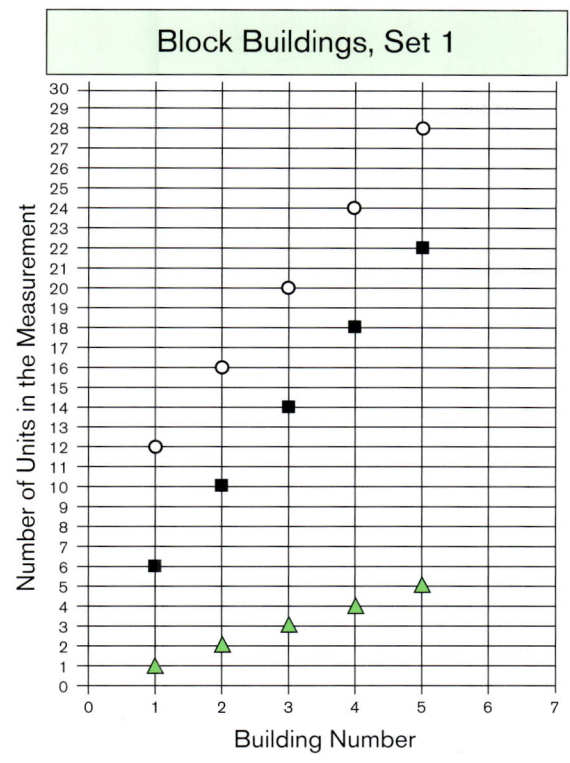
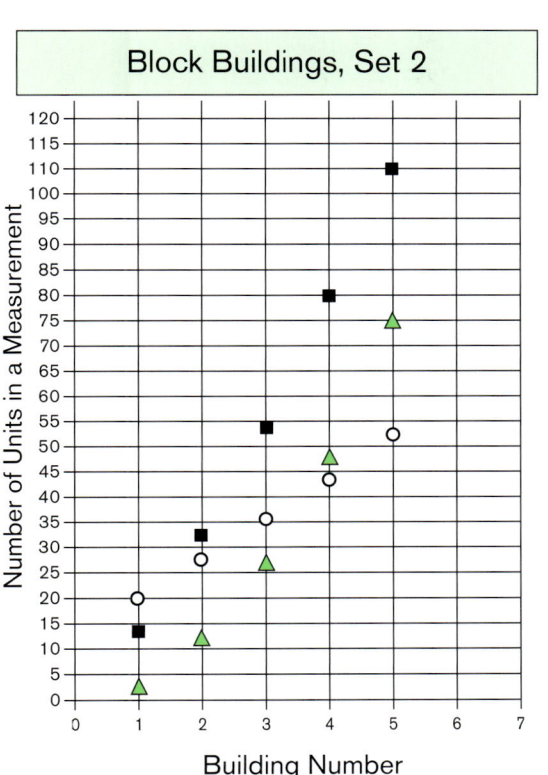
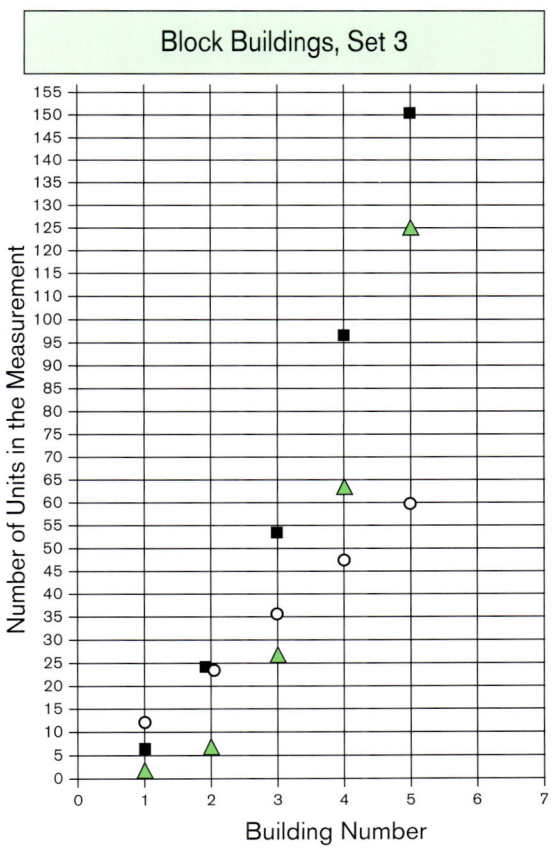

Fig. **10.**

Graphs of the measurements of the block buildings in sets 1, 2, and 3

You may wish to encourage your students to use graphing software or Web sites such as Spreadsheet and Graphing Calculator on the NCTM Illuminations Web site at http://illuminations.nctm.org/ActivityDetail.aspx?ID=38 or Graph Sketcher at http://www.shodor.org/interactivate/activities/sketcher/index.html.

are the same. Although both graphs are curves, the relationship of the surface areas represents a quadratic (second power) function, and the relationship of the volumes represents a cubic (third power) function. The rates of change for both the surface area and the volume are varying (increasing), but the volume is increasing much more rapidly.

In addition, the students may question why the graph of surface area shows linear growth in set 1 but nonlinear growth (quadratic relationships) in sets 2 and 3. Growth in the perimeter is linear in the graphs for all three sets. In contrast, growth in the volume is linear in the graph for set 1, quadratic in the graph for set 2, and cubic in the graph for set 3.

These differences depend directly on the number of dimensions that grow in a set of buildings. The buildings in set 1 grow in only one dimension (height), resulting in linear change in all three patterns—perimeter, surface area, and volume. The buildings in set 2 grow in two dimensions (length and width), while their heights are fixed at three units. In the graph for set 2, perimeter and surface area display the expected patterns of growth—linear in the case of perimeter, and quadratic in the case of surface area. In this case, volume is limited to quadratic rather than cubic growth, however, since growth from building to building in the set is only two-dimensional. The buildings in set 3 grow in all three dimensions—height, length, and width. Thus, the graphs of the three measurements reflect the units: the graph for perimeter is linear, that for surface area is quadratic (second power, showing a squaring), and that for volume is cubic (third power, showing a cubing).

*Extension*

Students can explore similar but more complex sets of block buildings to extend their understanding of growth in one, two, and three dimensions and of the functions associated with such growth. One approach is for them to determine if similar graphs result from the data for block buildings with other restrictions on the footprint and the height. They can, for instance, generate a table of data on perimeter, surface area, and volume for a set of buildings (set 1A) that have a fixed base of $1 \times 2$ square units and grow vertically. The structures and associated table are shown in figure 11. Values for the perimeters, surface areas, and volumes appear in the table, along with symbolic expressions for these measurements for building $n$. Note that all three patterns are linear, just as they were for set 1. When students compare sets 1 and 1A, they will see that the size of a constant footprint does not affect the linearity of patterns for sets of block buildings.

Figure 12 shows a set of buildings (set 2A) with a fixed height of 3 units and an increasing rectangular base. From one building to the next, both the length and width of the base increase by 1 unit ($1 \times 2$, $2 \times 3$, $3 \times 4$, etc.). The associated table gives values for the perimeters, surface areas, and volumes, along with symbolic expressions for these measurements for building $n$. Growth in the perimeter is linear, while growth in both the surface area and the volume is quadratic. When students compare sets 2 and 2A, they will see that the size of the base of building 1 does not affect the kind of curve displayed by the function for sets in which the height remains constant, but both width and length increase by constant amounts.

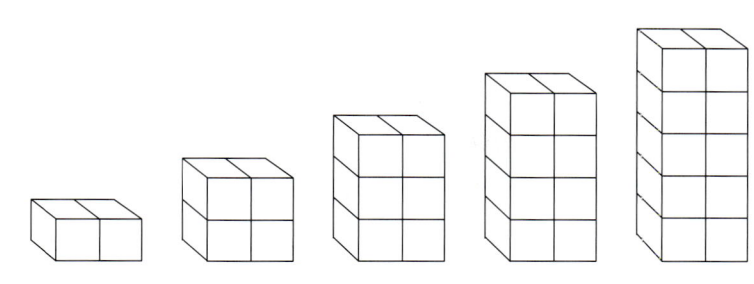

| Block Buildings, Set 1A | | | | | | |
|---|---|---|---|---|---|---|
| | Number of the Block Building | | | | | |
| | 1 | 2 | 3 | 4 | 5 | n |
| Perimeter (linear units) | 16 | 20 | 24 | 28 | 32 | 4n + 12, or 4(n + 3) |
| Surface area (square units) | 10 | 16 | 22 | 28 | 34 | 6n + 4, or 2(3n + 2) |
| Volume (cubic units) | 2 | 4 | 6 | 8 | 10 | 2n |

Fig. **11.**

A set of block buildings in which the footprint is held constant at 1 × 2 square units while the height increases from one building to the next

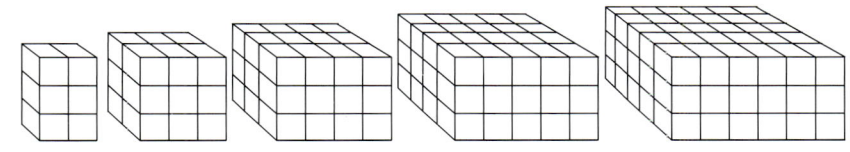

| Block Buildings, Set 2A | | | | | | |
|---|---|---|---|---|---|---|
| | Number of the Block Building | | | | | |
| | 1 | 2 | 3 | 4 | 5 | n |
| Perimeter (linear units) | 24 | 32 | 40 | 48 | 56 | 8n + 16, or 8(n + 2) |
| Surface area (square units) | 22 | 42 | 66 | 94 | 126 | $2n^2 + 14n + 6$ |
| Volume (cubic units) | 6 | 18 | 36 | 60 | 90 | 3n(n + 1) |

Fig. **12.**

A set of block buildings in which the height is held constant at three units while both the length and width increase from one building to the next

The students can compare set 3 with a set that begins with a rectangular structure whose dimensions are 1 × 2 × 3 and continues the pattern by adding one unit in each dimension for each succeeding building (2 × 3 × 4, 3 × 4 × 5, etc.). Figure 13 shows this set of buildings as set 3A, as well as an associated table of values for their perimeters, surface

 See Gregg (2002; available on the CD-ROM) for additional activities in which stacking cubes can be used to develop students' understanding of linear relationships.

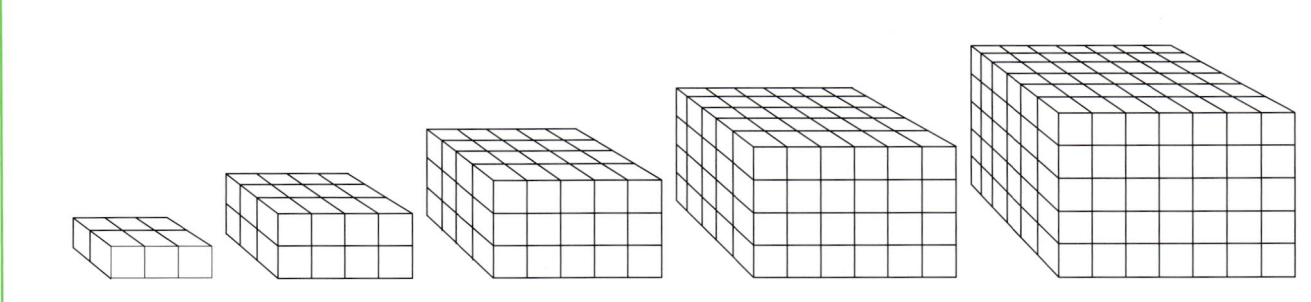

Fig. **13.**

A set of block buildings in which measurements in each dimension (height, length, and width) increase from one building to the next

| Block Buildings, Set 3A | | | | | | |
|---|---|---|---|---|---|---|
| | Number of the Block Building | | | | | |
| | 1 | 2 | 3 | 4 | 5 | $n$ |
| Perimeter (linear units) | 24 | 36 | 48 | 60 | 72 | $12n + 12$, or $12(n + 1)$ |
| Surface area (square units) | 22 | 52 | 94 | 148 | 214 | $6n^2 + 12n + 4$ |
| Volume (cubic units) | 6 | 24 | 60 | 120 | 210 | $n(n + 1)(n + 2)$, or $n^3 + 3n^2 + 2n$ |

areas, and volumes, with symbolic expressions for the measurements of building $n$. Growth in the perimeters, surface areas, and volumes of these buildings is linear, quadratic, and cubic, respectively.

## Assessment

Steps 1 and 2 on each activity sheet ask the students to construct sets of block buildings and record the perimeters, surface areas, and volumes of the structure in tables. Examine their completed tables to assess their abilities to organize and display data. Next, for each set, step 3 calls on the students to analyze the data to determine relationships between the measurements and the building numbers. If possible, the students write symbolic expressions or general (function) rules for the measurements of building $n$ in the case of each set. Evaluate your students' abilities to represent relationships and functions in words and mathematical symbols. Also use their work in this step to determine whether they can identify examples of a constant rate of change in the data. The students' work in steps 4–6 shows their abilities to create graphs and their understanding of the relationship between a data table and a graph of the same data. During the discussion of the graphs, listen for evidence that the students are aware of linear and nonlinear relationships and can recognize the relationships in graphs.

## Reflections

This investigation focuses on nonlinear and linear relationships while laying a foundation for an understanding of the significance of slope. These concepts are important in the study of algebra. As students explore patterns that exhibit such linear characteristics as a constant rate of change, they should reflect on the effects of the changes that occurred as they constructed the block buildings. For example, students should consider the impact of changes in height on the number of edges in the buildings (the perimeter), the area of the buildings (the surface area), and the total number of cubes that are both visible and invisible (the volume) in the buildings. They should discover in sets 2 and 3 that both the surface area and the volume have varying rates of change and that the volume increases much more rapidly than the other measurements, although its curve on the composite graph begins at a lower point than the curve for the surface area.

## Connections

Some of the most obvious connections in mathematics exist between geometry and algebra. This investigation takes advantage of these inherent connections by having students construct simple geometric structures—rectangular prisms—that grow according to given rules. The students quantify the growth by making measurements of the prisms' perimeters, surface areas, and volumes, and in the process, they collect data that they then display in tables and graphs. The students study the models, the data, and different representations of them to discover the relationships between the various measurements and the stage of growth. They express these relationships both in words and mathematical symbols. Through their work, they discover the power of tables and graphs as visual displays of change.

Measurement is an important component of this investigation. The students use centimeter cubes to build their block buildings, and they use an edge of a cube as the unit of linear measurement, the face of a cube as the unit to measure area, and the cube as the unit to measure volume. The measurement investigation, Scale Factors and Measurement Relationships (see p. 43) gives students another opportunity to compare the perimeters, areas, and volumes of figures. In that investigation, students discover that for two similar figures with a scale factor of $k$, the ratio of the perimeters is $k$ (linear), the ratio of the areas is $k^2$ (quadratic), and the ratio of the volumes is $k^3$ (cubic).

*The Measurement and Geometry Standards in* Principles and Standards for School Mathematics (NCTM 2000) *are connected with the Algebra Standards in investigations of such concepts as perimeter, area, and volume.*

# Understanding Area Formulas

## Focus

Reasoning about Geometric Relationships

## Overview

The activities in this investigation guide students in decomposing or performing transformations on parallelograms, triangles, and trapezoids to help them derive area formulas for these shapes. The goal is not for students to learn formulas but rather for them to learn methods of visualizing and of reasoning from visualizations to understand formulas. Other important goals of these activities are to help students understand the relationship between the dimensions of the shapes with which they begin and those that they derive and to ensure that they use the properties of shapes to make their visualized decompositions and transformations more precise.

After briefly reviewing the concept of area and the meanings of the terms *base*, *altitude*, and *height*, students decompose or transform shapes in tasks that enable them to derive and explain the area formulas for parallelograms, triangles, and trapezoids.

## Goals

- Make sense of area formulas by visualizing and reasoning carefully from visualizations
- Progress to higher levels of reasoning about decomposing and recomposing shapes
- Progress from thinking about shapes strictly visually to using measurement to approach them more analytically
- Reason informally about congruence and geometric transformations in applied situations
- Develop visualization skills

## Mathematical Content

Decomposing the interiors of two- and three-dimensional shapes in careful and analytic ways is an indispensable skill for reasoning about many mathematical problems. The development of this skill starts in the elementary grades and continues through calculus and beyond. In school, students decompose shapes to find their areas and volumes and understand fractional regions. Beyond the classroom, mathematicians, scientists, and engineers decompose shapes in their research and applications.

Understanding why formulas work is essential. Lacking such understanding, students may not realize when the formulas are applicable and when they are not, and they may develop a belief that mathematics

*Decomposing the interiors of two- and three-dimensional shapes in careful and analytic ways is an essential skill in reasoning about many mathematical problems.*

is primarily about procedural mimicry and memorization rather than sense making and conceptual understanding. Decomposing and composing shapes is the foundation for understanding area formulas. To decompose shapes and recompose the pieces in precise ways, students must understand and use appropriate length measurements, properties of shapes, and geometric manipulations.

This investigation directly or indirectly supports the following Geometry Standards and expectations for grades 6–8 (NCTM 2000, p. 397):

- Analyze characteristics and properties of two- and three-dimensional geometric shapes and develop mathematical arguments about geometric relationships
  - Precisely describe, classify, and understand relationships among types of [two-dimensional] ... objects using their defining properties
  - Understand relationships among the angles, side lengths ... [and] areas ... of similar objects
  - Create and critique inductive and deductive arguments concerning geometric ideas and relationships
- Apply transformations ... to analyze mathematical situations
  - Describe sizes, positions, and orientations of shapes under informal transformations such as flips, turns, [and] slides
  - Examine the congruence ... of objects using transformations
- Use visualization, spatial reasoning, and geometric modeling to solve problems
  - Draw geometric objects with specified properties, such as side lengths or angle measures
  - Use geometric models to represent and explain numerical and algebraic relationships

## Students' Mathematical Thinking

Research has produced convincing evidence that an effective way to improve mathematics instruction and learning is for teachers to understand the mathematical thought processes of their students (Fennema et al. 1996). A research-based knowledge of students' construction of meaning for core mathematical ideas can enhance teachers' understanding. For decomposing and recomposing shapes, research has identified several basic levels of sophistication in reasoning (Battista 2001).

### Level 1: Physical Decomposing and Recomposing

At this level, students have not sufficiently abstracted the images of shapes to visualize decomposing shapes and recomposing the pieces as other shapes. They have great difficulty in imagining how shapes can be decomposed, so they frequently imagine a decomposition inaccurately. To be successful, they must decompose and recompose shapes physically, mainly through trial and error. As students make the transition to level 2 thinking, they start to visualize possible decompositions and recompositions but must test their ideas by using concrete materials.

Understanding Area Formulas

### Level 2: Visualized Decomposing and Recomposing

Students at this level have abstracted the images of shapes well enough that they can mentally envision decomposing and recomposing them without the use of concrete materials. Students might still draw pictures to help them think about decompositions, although drawing decompositions of three-dimensional shapes can be quite difficult.

### Level 3: Visualized Decomposing and Recomposing with the Explicit Use of Measurement

At this level, students explicitly use measurements, in addition to visualization, to decompose and recompose shapes. They determine and compare areas by using measurement-guided decomposition. For instance, they use the lengths of sides to decide where to cut apart shapes and to decide if decomposed shapes are congruent.

## Prior Knowledge or Experience

- An understanding of area and why the area formula for a rectangle is accurate
- An introductory exposure to such concepts as lines, line segments, linear measurements, angles, congruence, slides, flips, and turns

## Materials

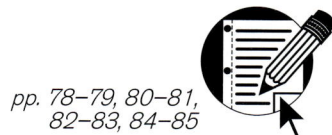

pp. 78–79, 80–81, 82–83, 84–85

For each student—
- A copy of each of the following activity sheets:
  - "Measuring Shapes"
  - "Make a Rectangle from That Parallelogram"
  - "Compare That Triangle with That Rectangle"
  - "Compare That Trapezoid with That Parallelogram"

For each pair of students—
- A ruler
- A pair of scissors
- Access to the 2-D Shape Decomposition Tool (optional; available on the accompanying CD-ROM)

For the teacher—
- Access to the 2-D Shape Decomposition Tool on a computer equipped with a large display device for whole-class viewing (optional)

## Classroom Environment

Throughout this investigation, each student works with a partner. Teachers should try to pair students of approximately equal mathematical ability.

## Investigation

Understanding Area Formulas consists of four tasks, each with its own activity sheet. At the beginning of each task, give every student a copy of the appropriate activity sheet. Pair the students, matching each one with a partner of approximately equal skill and understanding in mathematics, and tell all the students that they should discuss their thoughts with their partners as they work. Emphasize, however, that they should record their own ideas on their own activity sheets.

To progress to higher levels of reasoning about decomposing and transforming shapes, students need opportunities to visualize the decompositions, recompositions, or transformations necessary to solve a problem. Then they should use physical materials or, in this investigation, the electronic 2-D Shape Decomposition Tool, to check their proposed solutions. Be sure that your students find, record, and check each solution *before* they proceed to the next problem. Encourage them to discover additional solutions to a problem.

As the students explore solutions, opportunities will arise for them to use the concept of congruence, make transformations—including slides (translations) and turns (rotations)—name and describe polygons, and consider measurements. Often, however, students will use informal language to describe the concepts that they encounter and apply. For example, they may say "square corner" when describing a right angle, or they may talk about pieces that are "the same" when describing congruent shapes. When students use an informal term, introduce the formal one, define it, and demonstrate its meaning with drawings or classroom manipulatives. Teachers can often support students' conceptual development if they use *both* informal and formal terms until students become comfortable with the formal language.

Whether students use informal or formal terms, have them clarify the meaning of the terms that they use. If, for instance, students use the word *same* or *equal* for *congruent*, you can ask, "What do you mean when you say that those two shapes are the same [or equal]?" Students might respond that they can place one shape exactly on top of the other shape, covering it exactly and completely. You can push students to sharpen their thinking by asking, "When two shapes are the same, or *congruent*, what do you know about their sides and angles?" Help students see that corresponding sides and angles (those that fit over each other if the two shapes coincide) of congruent shapes are themselves congruent.

As the students work on a task, circulate among them, and have them explain and justify their work. Ask them why some attempts at solutions fail and others succeed. Carefully observe how the students are solving problems. Which details are the focus of their attention? How are they making the decompositions and recompositions? Do they match pieces of shapes according to side lengths or angle measures? Do they use the properties of shapes to help compare them? Record your observations of students' strategies so that you can use them both for assessment and as topics for discussion in follow-up instruction.

After the students have completed a task, guide them in sharing and discussing their solutions, methods, and reasoning. To facilitate the discussion, record various solutions on a transparency, or recreate them with the 2-D Shape Decomposition Tool and display them with an appropriate projection device. Allow time for the students to evaluate one another's solutions. Encourage them to share a variety of ideas— even those that were unsuccessful. Ask the students to explain how they

Teachers can often support students' conceptual development if they use *both* informal and formal terms until students become comfortable with the formal language.

*To progress to higher levels of reasoning about decomposing and transforming shapes, students need opportunities to visualize the decompositions, recompositions, or transformations necessary to solve a problem.*

Understanding Area Formulas

Some textbooks define a *trapezoid* as a quadrilateral that has *at least* one pair of opposite sides parallel. By that definition, parallelograms are a special type of trapezoid. By the definition that the Navigations Series uses, however, parallelograms are not trapezoids.

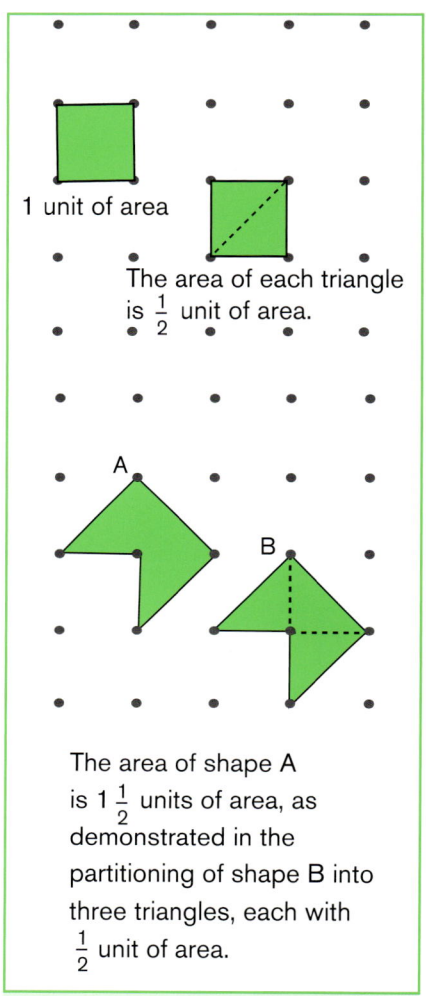

Fig. **14.**

Finding the area of a shape

Fig. **15.**

Students work with a rectangle partitioned into four rows of squares, with five squares in each row, to explain the area formula for a rectangle.

found solutions and—more important—why they believe their solutions are correct or how they determined that they were incorrect. Encourage them to develop convincing explanations of their solutions. This investigation allows for considerable variation in mathematical rigor. The discussions of the tasks suggest ways to extend them for students who would benefit from a greater challenge than the basic tasks afford. Assess your students' readiness for increased rigor on the basis of their mathematics backgrounds.

### Task 1—Measuring Shapes

The activity sheet "Measuring Shapes" briefly reviews the notions of area, base, altitude, and height. Before giving each student a copy of the sheet, ask the students what they know about quadrilaterals, rectangles, parallelograms, and trapezoids. Pose questions to elicit the following properties of shapes:

- A quadrilateral is a four-sided polygon.
- A rectangle is a quadrilateral with four right angles.
- A parallelogram is a quadrilateral with both pairs of opposite sides parallel. The opposite sides are congruent (that is, the same length), as are the opposite angles. Pairs of adjacent angles are supplementary (in other words, their measures sum to 180°).
- A trapezoid is a quadrilateral that has exactly one pair of parallel sides. The parallel sides are the *bases* of the trapezoid.

*Area.* The area of a region is the number of area units needed to fill the region with no gaps or overlaps. Area units are usually squares, so they are called square units. Ask the students to name some common area units. They might suggest square centimeters, square inches, square feet, square yards, square meters, or square miles. Some students will probably think only about whole units, so remind the class that to determine area, unit squares can be cut or deformed (see fig. 14 for an example of using halves of a unit).

The activity sheet "Measuring Shapes" relates the concepts *base*, *altitude*, and *height* specifically to triangles, parallelograms, and trapezoids. Distribute the sheet and let the students begin work. Steps 1–3 review why the area formula for a rectangle yields a correct measurement. Help the students see that the length represents the number of squares in each row of a rectangle ($l = 5$ in fig. 15), and the width represents the number of rows ($w = 4$ in fig. 15). Multiplying the length by the width gives the total number of unit squares ($5 \times 4 = 20$).

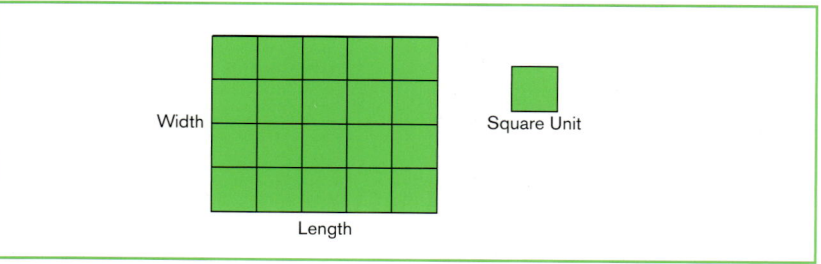

***Base, Altitude, and Height.*** Steps 4–6 help the students clarify and apply some terminology related to triangles, parallelogram, and trapezoids. The terms *base*, *altitude*, and *height* are necessary for describing the dimensions of these shapes, in which the height is the length of an altitude.

Any side of a triangle can be its base. The altitude for the chosen base is the line segment that is perpendicular to the base and joins a point on it, or an extension of it, to the opposite vertex. Thus, the altitude does not necessarily intersect the base. Some altitudes are inside the triangle, as in figure 16a, and some are outside, as in figure 16b. Only one altitude can be drawn from each base or an extension of it; hence, a triangle has three altitudes. A base can have any orientation. However, to facilitate students' visualizations, the base always appears in a horizontal orientation in the examples on the activity sheet.

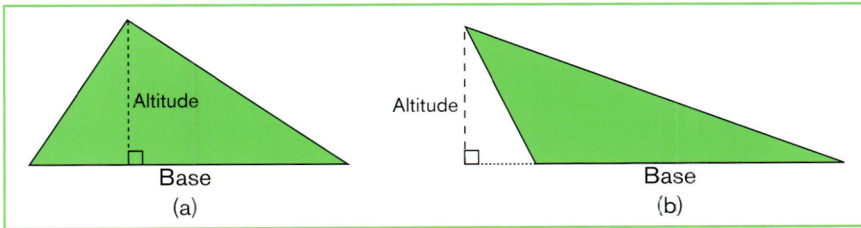

Fig. 16.

An altitude of a triangle may be interior (a) or exterior (b).

Any side of a parallelogram can be its base. The altitude for a chosen base is a line segment that is perpendicular to the base and joins a point on it, or on a extension of it, to the opposite side, or an extension of it. Unless a parallelogram is a rectangle, some altitudes are inside the parallelogram, and some are outside (see fig. 17). Each parallelogram has an infinite number of altitudes but a maximum of two distinct heights.

The base of a trapezoid can be either of its parallel sides. An altitude of the chosen base is a line segment that is perpendicular to the base and joins a point on it, or an extension of it, to the opposite side, or an extension of it. Some altitudes are inside the trapezoid, and some are outside (see fig. 18). Each trapezoid has an infinite number of altitudes but only one distinct height.

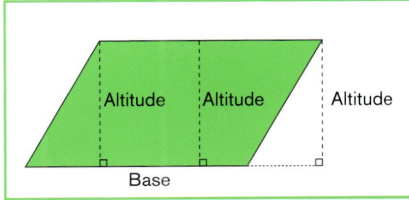

Fig. 17.

A parallelogram has an infinite number of altitudes, which may be interior or exterior.

### Task 2—Make a Rectangle from That Parallelogram

Before beginning task 2, review transformations with your students. They should understand what translating, rotating, and reflecting shapes involve:

- A *translation* slides a shape to a new position without changing its orientation. (A translation is also called a *slide*.)
- A *rotation* pivots a shape on a fixed point. (A rotation is also called a *turn*.)
- A *reflection* flips a shape over a *line of reflection* to create a mirror image. (A reflection is also called a *flip*.)

On the board, draw a trapezoid like that in figure 18, and call on students to demonstrate a slide, a turn, and a flip. Remind the class that under any of these transformations the image of a shape is congruent to the original shape, which is sometimes called the *preimage*.

Give each student a copy of the activity sheet "Make a Rectangle from That Parallelogram." Step 1 shows four parallelograms and asks the students to draw a line segment on each to divide it into two pieces that they could rearrange to form a rectangle. They should make marks on the drawings to show how they would form the rectangles that they have in mind.

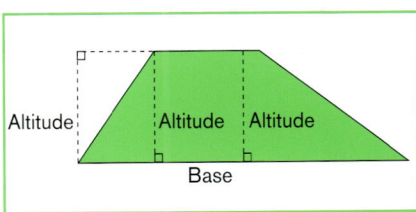

Fig. 18.

A trapezoid has an infinite number of altitudes, which may be interior or exterior.

**Understanding Area Formulas**

Note that step 1 simplifies the exercise by telling the students to place all the end points of their dividing segments on dots in the square grid. In addition, the orientation of the examples ensures that each dividing segment will be either vertical or horizontal. In general, however, parallelograms and dividing segments can have any orientation. Before continuing to step 2, the students should check each answer in step 1 by cutting out the parallelogram, slicing it, and rearranging the pieces by hand or by using the 2-D Shape Decomposition Tool to accomplish the same result.

Fig. **19.**

Altitude *XY* cuts parallelogram *ABCD* to form trapezoids *ABYX* and *XYCD*. Trapezoid *ABYX* slides "down" to form rectangle *XYQP*.

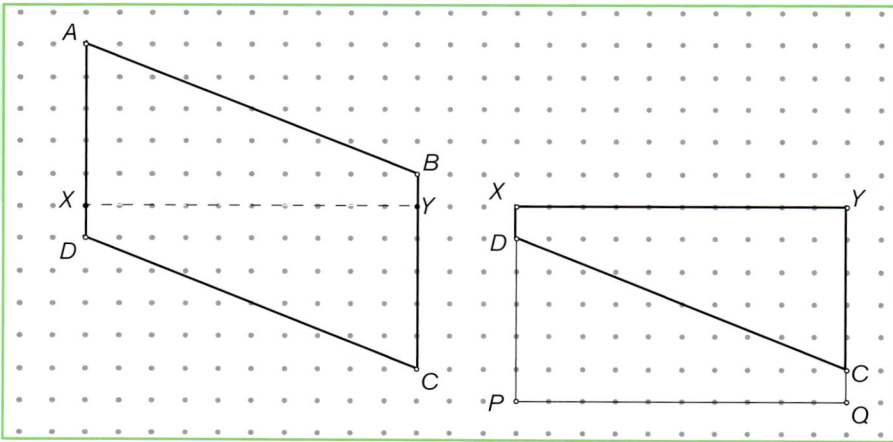

In step 2, the students use the same process of decomposition, transformation, and recomposition as in step 1, but the new problem supplies no grid to help them decide where to cut the given parallelogram. They must choose a base and draw a segment that is perpendicular to it and intersects the opposite side of the parallelogram. Figure 20 shows one such solution.

Fig. **20.**

One way to cut a parallelogram to make a rectangle

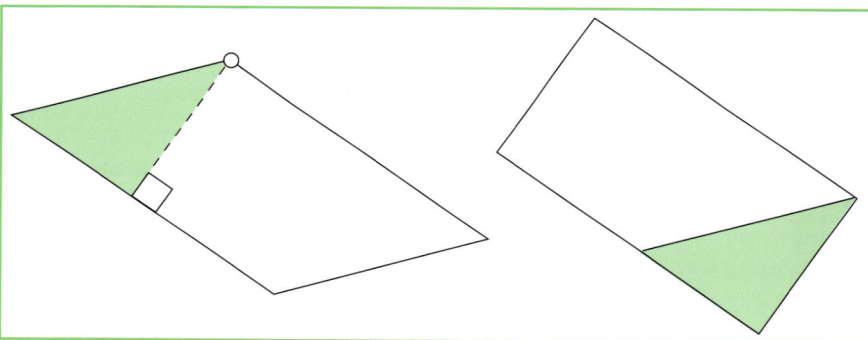

In step 2, it is important that students understand that a dividing segment must be perpendicular to the chosen base and intersect the opposite side—that is, the dividing segment must be an altitude. When the students say that their dividing segment is perpendicular to the base, ask them how they know that it is perpendicular. They might demonstrate the perpendicularity informally by rotating the parallelogram so that the base is horizontal and the segment appears to be vertical.

Ask the students how they might convince others that this visual solution is correct. One method would be to measure the angle formed by the segment and the base to show that it is a 90-degree angle. An informal way to "measure" a right angle is to use the corner of an index card to show that the angle is the same as that of the corner of the card. Students whose reasoning is more advanced are likely to use angle measure first—to draw a perpendicular segment—instead of afterward—to check the measurement when you or someone else challenges them.

In step 3, students use their work in steps 1 and 2 to help them explain the area formula for a parallelogram:

*Area = base × height.*

They should argue that they could cut any parallelogram into two pieces by drawing an appropriate altitude. Then they could slide one of the pieces to the other side of the parallelogram to form a rectangle (see fig. 21). Because they would be neither adding nor taking away any area in the process of decomposing, sliding, and recomposing, the resulting rectangle would have the same area as the original parallelogram. To find the area of this rectangle, they would multiply its length by its width. The length and width of the rectangle would be, respectively, the length of the base and the height of the parallelogram.

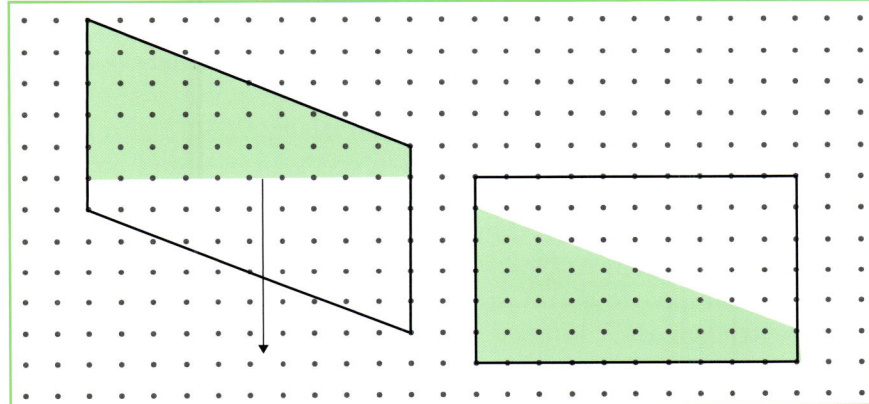

**Fig. 21.**

Slide the top part of the parallelogram down to form a rectangle.

## Task 3—Compare That Triangle with That Rectangle

Rectangles, and the formula for the area of a rectangle, continue to be important in task 3. Task 2 helped students explore the area of a parallelogram by decomposing a given parallelogram and rearranging the parts to form a rectangle of equal area. In task 3, they explore the area of a triangle by relating it to the area of a particular rectangle. For any given triangle, they draw a rectangle that shares a base with the triangle and includes its remaining vertex as a point on the rectangle's opposite side. For example, in figure 22, rectangle *ABDE* shares side *AB* with triangle *ABC*, and the triangle's remaining vertex, *C*, is a point on the opposite side (*ED*) of the rectangle. The rectangle has twice the area of the original triangle, offering a basis for the idea that the area of a triangle is equal to one-half of its base times its height.

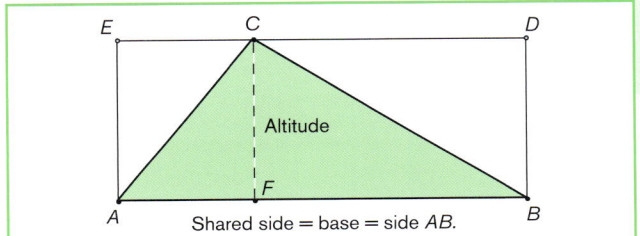

**Fig. 22.**

Rectangle *ABDE* has twice the area of triangle *ABC*.

Give each student a copy of the activity sheet "Compare That Triangle with That Rectangle" and again let the students work in pairs. The aim of the exercise is for the students to notice that the areas of the triangles are always one-half of the areas of the corresponding rectangles that they draw. Once they recognize this fact, they use it to explain the area formula for a triangle:

$$Area = \frac{1}{2} (base \times height).$$

To simplify the problems, each triangle appears on a dot grid. All three of the triangle's vertices are on grid dots, and the triangle is oriented so that one of its sides aligns horizontally or vertically with the grid. This is the side that students should use as the base that the triangle shares with the rectangle that they draw. All sides of this rectangle will thus be horizontal or vertical line segments terminating on grid dots. Consequently, the area of the rectangle will be easy to determine. In general, of course, triangles can appear in any orientation.

For each rectangle that the students draw, they should recognize that the area of the original triangle is one-half the area of the corresponding rectangle. To show that this is so, they can cut out each rectangle and remove the two right triangles that the rectangle's construction adds to the area of the original triangle. In figure 22, for example, triangle *ACE* could be placed on top of triangle *CAF*, and triangle *BDC* on top of triangle *CFB*, to show that the triangles in each pair are congruent, and thus, the area of triangle *ABC* is half of the area of rectangle *ABDE*.

Alternatively, the students can use the 2-D Shape Decomposition Tool on the CD-ROM to show this fact. They can make the cuts to decompose rectangle *ABDE* into triangle *ACE*, *ABC*, and *BDC*. Then they can rotate triangle *ACE* 180 degrees about the midpoint of line segment *AC* onto triangle *CAF* and rotate triangle *BDC* 180 degrees about the midpoint of segment *BC* onto triangle *CFB*.

A more rigorous argument that the area of the triangle is one-half the area of the rectangle depends on demonstrating that *ABDE* is in fact a rectangle—not just a figure that looks like a rectangle. Most students will draw the rectangle with a pencil and straightedge. However, if the students have studied the angle properties of perpendicular and parallel lines, you can make—or ask them to make—more precise drawings to demonstrate that what they have drawn is a rectangle.

To demonstrate that *ABDE* is a rectangle, construct line *m* perpendicular to side *AB* at *A* and line *n* perpendicular to *AB* at *B*. Through *C*, construct line *p* parallel to side *AB* (see fig. 23). Let *E* be the point of intersection of *p* and *m*, and let *D* be the intersection of *p* and *n*. Explain that because line segment *DE* is parallel to line segment *AB*, line segment *AE* is perpendicular to line segment *DE*, since same-side interior angles of parallel lines cut by a *transversal* are supplementary. (A transversal is a line that intersects two or more lines in a plane at different points. Angle *BAE* is 90 degrees, so angle *DEA* is also 90 degrees; 90 + 90 = 180.) Similarly, line segment *DB* is perpendicular to side *DE*. So all four angles of quadrilateral *ABDE* are right angles, and thus, by definition, *ABDE* is a rectangle.

Even if your students cannot give a rigorous argument, the following question can be worthwhile: "How do you know that what you drew is really a rectangle—is it possible that it just looks like a rectangle?" Students may give informal versions of the preceding argument.

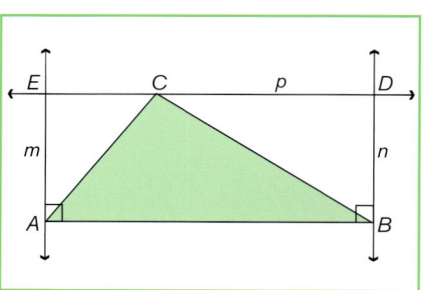

**Fig. 23.**

Constructing lines *m* and *n* perpendicular to segment *AB*, and line *p* parallel to *AB*, supports an argument that *ABDE* is a rectangle.

In step 2, the students use the same process of exploring a triangle's area by drawing a rectangle that shares a side with the triangle and includes the triangle's remaining vertex as a point in the rectangle's opposite side. However, the triangle in this step does not appear on a grid (see fig. 24). In addition, the new triangle is obtuse—that is, one of its angles is greater than 90 degrees. All the triangles in step 1 are acute or right triangles.

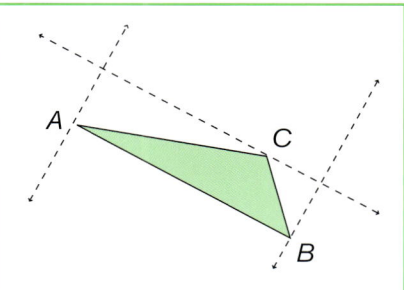

Fig. 24.

The "corresponding rectangle" for the triangle in step 2

The construction process outlined above suggests how the students can solve the new problem. But first they must choose a side of the triangle to be the shared base of the triangle and rectangle. Because the new triangle, labeled *ABC* in the figure, is obtuse, this side must be *AB*—the only side with acute angles at both vertices. Neither of the other sides permits the construction of a rectangle by the process that the students have used in the activity. After selecting *AB* as the base, they then construct lines through points *A* and *B* that are perpendicular to it. Finally, they draw a line through point *C* parallel to side *AB* to form a rectangle.

If your students' geometric reasoning is more advanced, you might ask them why they cannot choose either of the other sides of the triangle as the base of the rectangle. See if they understand that the construction of the rectangle requires an altitude that divides the original triangle into two right triangles. If the angle at one end of the base of the original triangle is obtuse, the altitude to that base is outside the triangle.

You might also ask the students why it is possible, in *any* triangle, to find one side that has acute angles at both ends. Can they see that the only way that a triangle would not have such a side would be if at least two of the angles of the triangle were obtuse. But such a situation is impossible, because the sum of the angles of the triangle would then exceed 180 degrees.

The students follow the same process of comparison as before to see that the area of the triangle in step 2 is half of the area of the rectangle that they draw. Figure 25 shows the original triangle, with vertices labeled *ABC*, and the constructed rectangle, with vertices *ABDE*. The figure labels four triangles formed by the sides of the rectangle, the sides of the original triangle, and the altitude of the original triangle from base *AB*.

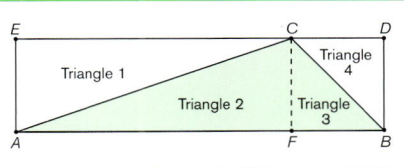

Fig. 25.

Comparing the areas of a triangle and its corresponding rectangle

Triangles 1 and 2 are congruent (rotating one triangle 180° about the midpoint of *AC* covers the other triangle exactly), so their areas are equal. Therefore, the area of triangle 1 plus the area of triangle 2 is equal to two times the area of triangle 2. Similarly, the areas of triangles 3 and 4 are equal. So the area of triangle 3 plus the area of triangle 4 is equal to two times the area of triangle 3. Thus, the students can see that

Area of rectangle *ABDE*

> = area of triangle 1 + area of triangle 2 + area of triangle 3 + area of triangle 4
>
> = 2(area of triangle 2) + 2(area of triangle 3)
>
> = 2(area of triangle 2 + area of triangle 3)
>
> = 2(area of triangle *ABC* ).

Understanding Area Formulas

Therefore,
$$\text{Area of triangle } ABC = \frac{1}{2} (\text{area of rectangle } ABDE).$$

Help the students see the logic of this argument, but don't expect them to be able to construct the argument step by step themselves. Your students may give an informal version of this proof, usually by pointing to parts of the figure rather than using the customary labels for the angles and sides of the figures. Or they might, for instance, cut out rectangle *ABDE* in figure 25 and then cut it apart along segments *AC* and *BC* so that they can lay triangle *ACE* on triangle *CAF* and triangle *BCD* on triangle *CBF*.

In step 3, students should integrate their thinking from steps 1 and 2 to formulate an argument that justifies the area formula for a triangle. Their explanations will vary but should make the same basic argument: For any triangle, they can draw a corresponding rectangle that shares a base with the triangle, has the same altitude as the triangle, and has twice the area of the triangle. Therefore, because the area of the rectangle is the length of the base times the height, the area of the triangle is $\frac{1}{2}$ of the length of the base times the height.

### Task 4—Compare That Trapezoid with That Parallelogram

In task 4, the students explore the areas of trapezoids. They again apply techniques of transformation, decomposition, and recomposition, this time to compare the area of a given trapezoid with that of a parallelogram constructed in a particular way. Give each student a copy of the activity sheet "Compare that Trapezoid with That Parallelogram." Guide the students through the opening section, which calls their attention to a pictured trapezoid and asks them to imagine forming a related parallelogram through the following steps:

1. Make an exact copy of the trapezoid.
2. Place it on top of the original trapezoid, with congruent sides and angles aligned.
3. Put a pin through both the original and the copy precisely at the midpoint of one of the nonparallel sides.
4. Rotate the copy one-half turn (180 degrees).

The trapezoid and its *rotation image* would then form a parallelogram (see fig. 26).

Let the students begin work on the task, again in pairs. Step 1 presents two trapezoids and asks them to construct related parallelograms

Drawings for tasks 3 and 4 can be made with the Geometer's Sketchpad.

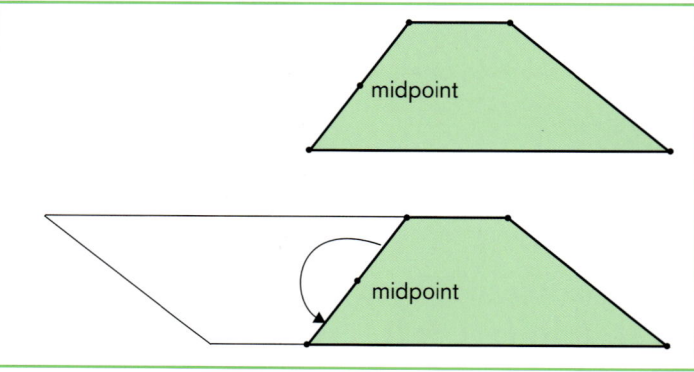

Fig. **26.**
Rotating a trapezoid to demonstrate that the original trapezoid and its rotation image form a parallelogram

by using the process described above. The students should realize that in each case two different parallelograms are possible, since a trapezoid has two nonparallel sides. They should also see, however, that these parallelograms have the same base and same height and therefore the same area. Moreover, because the rotated trapezoid is congruent to the original trapezoid, the two trapezoids—preimage and rotation image—have equal area. Therefore, the area of each parallelogram is twice the area of the original trapezoid.

After the students have drawn a parallelogram for each trapezoid in step 1, they consider how its area compares with that of the trapezoid and test their ideas by various methods. They can cut out each parallelogram and decompose it into trapezoids that they can place one on top of the other to demonstrate their congruence. Alternatively, they can work with the 2-D Shape Decomposition Tool to probe the relationship between the original trapezoid and the parallelogram formed by the trapezoid and its rotation image. The students should draw the imagined parallelogram before performing the rotation.

After the experimentation in step 1, step 2 asks the students to explain the area formula for a trapezoid. Note that the argument given above explains why parallelogram *BCEF* in figure 27 has twice the area of trapezoid *BCDA*. Finding the area of the original trapezoid (*BCDA*) simply requires determining the area of parallelogram *BCEF* and taking half of it. Because trapezoid *EFAD* is the rotation image of the original trapezoid, the two trapezoids are congruent. So side *FA*, the rotation image of side *CD*, is the same length as side *CD*. Similarly, side *ED* is the same length as side *BA*. Therefore, the length of parallelogram side *FB* is the length of base 1 of the original trapezoid plus the length of base 2. On the basis of their work in task 2, the students know that the area of the parallelogram is (length of base 1 + length of base 2) times the height. They can therefore explain that the area of a trapezoid is equal to one-half of the area of parallelogram formed by the trapezoid and its rotation image, which means that for any trapezoid,

$$Area = \frac{1}{2} (base\ 1 + base\ 2) \times height.$$

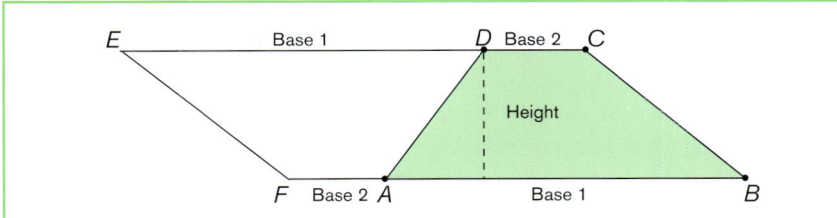

Fig. 27.

Finding the area of the parallelogram formed from a trapezoid and its rotation image

Showing rigorously that the figure formed in task 4 by a trapezoid and its rotation image is a parallelogram is beyond the ability of most sixth graders. Nevertheless, you can ask questions to help your students increase the precision of their arguments. For instance, you can show them such a parallelogram, labeled as in figure 27, and say, "We know that in a parallelogram, opposite sides and opposite angles are congruent. Show that this statement is true for figure *EFBC*." The students might notice that opposite angles in *EFBC* are congruent because they are rotation images of each other. The same is true of sides *EF* and *BC*. We have already shown that both horizontal sides of the parallelogram have length equal to (length of base 1 + length of base 2), so they are

**Understanding Area Formulas**

congruent. In a completely rigorous proof, we would also have to show that segments *ED* and *DC* are on the same line.

## Assessment

As you circulate among your students at work, listen closely as they explain and justify their ideas. Pay attention to their thoughts about why some solution attempts fail and others succeed. Observe what they are noticing as they make the decompositions, transformations, and recompositions. Do they talk about, and take account of, side lengths or angle measures? Do they consider properties of shapes to help them compare them? Relate the information that you gather to the levels of reasoning about decomposition and recomposition described at the beginning of this investigation.

## Reflections

The goal of this investigation is not only to help students make sense of area formulas but also to involve them in two important types of mathematical reasoning. First, students use *visualization* to make inferences about area. Second, they use *deductive reasoning* to derive the formula for one shape from the formula for another shape whose area formula is already known. This type of reasoning—solving a problem by using a problem that has already been solved—is fundamental in mathematics. Thus, in addition to introducing students to important mathematical procedures for finding area, the tasks strengthen students' mathematical reasoning. Perhaps most important, these activities not only help students make sense of mathematics but also demonstrate to them that mathematics makes sense.

As students encounter other tasks like those in this investigation, their abilities to visualize and reason about shapes will continue to develop. By integrating these skills with their expanding knowledge of length, angle measures, properties of shapes, and other geometric concepts, they will become more proficient in their analyses of shapes.

The geometry investigations in *Navigating through Problem Solving and Reasoning in Grade 3* (Yeatts et al. 2004) and *Navigating through Problem Solving and Reasoning in Grade 4* (Yeatts et al. 2005) also involve decomposing and recomposing shapes to develop similar skills of reasoning about two-dimensional shapes. Visualization and analytic reasoning about three-dimensional shapes are the focus of the geometry investigation in *Navigating through Problem Solving and Reasoning in Grade 5* (Thompson et al. 2007). These units can serve as resources to support your students' work on reasoning about shapes.

## Connections

Decomposing and recomposing regions in increasingly rigorous ways and describing decompositions algebraically by formulas are essential components of both geometric and algebraic reasoning. For additional work on these ideas, see the geometry investigations in the *Navigating through Problem Solving and Reasoning* books for grades 3–5 (Yeatts et al. 2004, Yeatts et al. 2005, Thompson et al. 2007) and the Area Formulas lesson on NCTM's Illuminations Web site.

---

The Area Formulas lesson on the Illuminations Web site (http://illuminations.nctm.org/LessonDetail.aspx?id=U160) offers additional ideas and possibilities for students.

Flores (2006) discusses using technology to teach area formulas, and Pagni (2006/2007) presents ideas for investigating area formulas with dot paper.

# Scale Factors and Measurement Relationships

## Focus

Reasoning about measurement relationships

## Overview

Sixth-grade students are likely to have had many everyday experiences with similar figures, even if they have not recognized them as such. For instance, most children have played with toys that are scale models of actual objects. Model trains and dolls are obvious examples. A number of films involve scale relationships, including *Honey! I Shrunk the Kids* and the Harry Potter and Lord of the Rings series of movies. Many classic stories and folktales involve elves or giants who are similar to ordinary humans but on a much smaller or larger scale. Students often enlarge or shrink an image on a computer screen or copy machine. They have probably also seen scale models that architects construct for proposed buildings by applying scale factors to the dimensions of the planned structures.

Activities that focus on measurement relationships among similar figures offer middle-grades students opportunities to explore ideas related to proportional reasoning, a topic that occupies a large part of the middle-grades mathematics curriculum. The activities in this investigation do not involve simply equating two ratios and solving for a missing term. Rather, they require students to recognize "quantities that are related proportionally and using numbers, tables, graphs, and equations to think about the quantities and their relationship" (NCTM 2000, p. 217). Early, often informal experiences with proportional reasoning should prove helpful to students as they explore increasingly abstract proportional relationships in middle school, where they work with linear functions of the form $y = kx$.

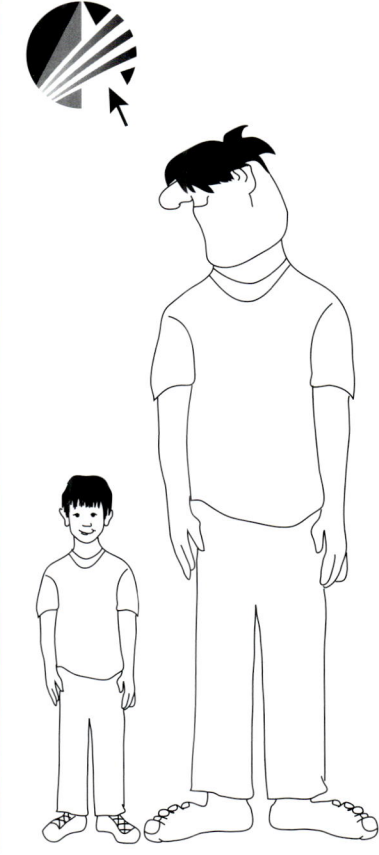

## Goals

- Use scale factors to construct figures that are similar to a given figure
- Compare the perimeters, areas, and volumes of similar figures
- Determine how the perimeters, areas, and volumes of similar figures are related to their scale factors
- Use the relationships between the perimeters, the areas, and the volumes of similar figures to solve real-world problems
- Determine the scale factor from measurements that are equivalent according to a scale, such as "1 inch equals 25 miles" on a map

## Mathematical Content

In this investigation, students begin with two- or three-dimensional figures and construct similar figures by applying a given scale factor. Multiplying all the dimensions of the original figure (called the *preimage*) by the same scale factor produces a new figure (called the *image*) that is similar to the original. The new figure is also commonly called a *size change*, or *dilation*, of the original. When the scale factor is greater than 1, the resulting figure is an enlargement of the original; when the scale factor is between 0 and 1, the resulting figure is a contraction, or reduction, of the original.

Throughout the three tasks in this investigation, students have opportunities to construct similar figures by using a given scale factor. For two-dimensional figures, they determine the lengths of corresponding sides of the preimage and the image, as well as the perimeters and areas of the figures. For three-dimensional figures, they determine the surface areas and volumes of the preimage and image. By determining the ratios of the corresponding sides, perimeters, areas, and volumes of the figures, students detect patterns and describe relationships in terms of the scale factor. They can use proportional reasoning to determine the perimeter, area, or volume of a figure if they know the dimensions of a figure that is similar to it as well as the scale factor for the relationship between the two figures.

When the students explore surface areas and volumes of similar figures in this investigation, they use centimeter cubes to build rectangular prisms, as they did in the algebra investigation, Block Buildings. However, the rules for sets 1 and 2 in the earlier investigation held at least one dimension of the block prisms constant while the others increased, so the resulting structures were not similar. The students looked for patterns and wrote rules for the changing perimeters, surface areas, and volumes of the figures, but proportional reasoning did not play a role in that earlier work. Nevertheless, that investigation and this one are natural complements and together can reinforce students' understanding of the ideas in each.

The new investigation incorporates the following Standards and expectations from *Principles and Standards for School Mathematics* (NCTM 2000, pp. 393–99, 402) for grades 6–8:

*Measurement*
- Understand, select, and use units of appropriate size ... to measure ... perimeter, area, surface area, and volume
- Develop strategies to determine the surface areas and volumes of selected prisms
- Solve problems involving scale factors, using ratio and proportion

*Geometry*
- Understand relationships among the ... side lengths, perimeters, areas, and volumes of similar objects

*Algebra*
- Represent, analyze, and generalize a variety of patterns with tables, graphs, words, and, when possible, symbolic rules

*Number and Operations*
- Understand and use ratios and proportions to represent quantitative relationships

- Develop, analyze, and explain methods for solving problems involving proportions, such as scaling and finding equivalent ratios

*Problem Solving*
- Build new mathematical knowledge through problem solving
- Solve problems that arise in mathematics and in other contexts

*Reasoning and Proof*
- Make and investigate mathematical conjectures

*Communication*
- Use the language of mathematics to express mathematical ideas precisely

*Representation*
- Create and use representations to organize, record, and communicate mathematical ideas

## Prior Knowledge or Experience

- An understanding of the concepts of perimeter, area, and volume
- Experience in finding the perimeters and areas of figures drawn on a dot grid
- Experience in finding the surface areas and volumes of rectangular prisms
- Experience in writing and simplifying ratios

## Materials

For each student, pair, or group of students—
- A copy of each of the following activity sheets:
  - "Scale It Up, Scale It Down"
  - "Perimeters and Areas of Similar Figures"
  - "Surface Areas and Volumes of Similar Figures"
  - "Scale Models"
- One or two sheets of quarter-inch grid paper (template on the CD-ROM)
- 150 centimeter cubes or other small cubes
- A calculator (scientific or four-function)

For the teacher—
- A transparency of the activity sheet "Scale It Up, Scale It Down" (optional)
- An overhead projector (optional)
- One or more of the following children's books (optional):
  *Gulliver's Adventures in Lilliput* (Beneduce 1996)
  *Jim and the Beanstalk* (Briggs 1997)

*Using tasks that address multiple benchmarks and several strands is one strategy to maximize curriculum coverage within the time constraints of the school year.*

*The Measurement and Geometry Standards from* Principles and Standards for School Mathematics *(NCTM 2000) are intertwined in the study of concepts such as similarity, perimeter, area, and volume.*

*pp. 86, 87–89, 90–91, 92–94*

You can use the template "Quarter-Inch Grid Paper" on the CD-ROM to print sheets of paper for your students' use in the investigation.

Numerous works of children's literature involve scales and ratios; the titles identified in the materials list are annotated in the reference section. Before each task in the investigation, consider reading one such work. Although it may not focus on comparisons of the respective perimeters, areas, or volumes of similar figures, it may be useful in introducing the ideas and motivating students to think about them.

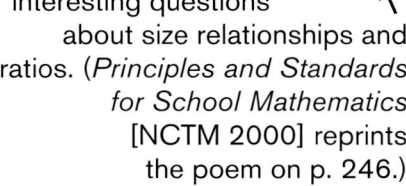

Shel Silverstein's poem "One Inch Tall" (1974) also raises interesting questions about size relationships and ratios. (*Principles and Standards for School Mathematics* [NCTM 2000] reprints the poem on p. 246.)

*Students in the middle grades should make and investigate mathematical conjectures. Teachers need to provide tasks that allow students to explore mathematical concepts and develop conjectures based on their investigations.*

*Gilliver in Lilliput* (Hodges 1995)
*Beanstalk: The Measure of a Giant* (McCallum 2006)
*If You Hopped like a Frog* (Schwartz 1999)
*If Dogs Were Dinosaurs* (Schwartz 2005)
*Cut Down to Size at High Noon* (Sundby 2000)
*Issunboshi* (Suyeoko, Goodman, and Spicer 1974)

## Classroom Environment

Depending on the task, students can work individually, in pairs, or in small groups. Students can easily complete task 1 (Perimeters and Areas of Similar Figures) individually, since all students should be able to construct the dilations on the activity sheet "Scale It Up, Scale It Down." In task 2 (Surface Areas and Volumes of Similar Figures), working in pairs or groups of three allows the students to help one another build the rectangular prisms. (Group work also economizes on the number of centimeter cubes, or other small cubes, for the class.) Students can complete task 3 (Scale Models) individually, in pairs, or in small groups, depending on the teacher's preference. It is important to discuss the results of students' work on each task in a whole-class setting.

## Investigation

As students move from the elementary to the middle grades, they should apply their earlier measurement experiences with perimeter, area, and volume as they reason about relationships between two similar figures. Students should discover that applying a scale factor to every dimension of an initial figure allows the formation of another figure that is an enlargement or a reduction of the original. That scale factor is the basis of the relationships between the respective perimeters, areas, and volumes of the two similar figures.

Because many situations involve scale factors, it is natural to wonder how the corresponding perimeters, areas, and volumes compare in two figures whose dimensions differ by a scale factor. Many students initially have misconceptions about the relationships between corresponding measurements in similar figures. This investigation comprises three tasks; each one focuses on a different aspect of scale factors and the measurements of similar figures formed by applying a given scale factor to the original figure. The purpose of the investigation is to enable students to compare the corresponding perimeters, areas, and volumes of similar figures and understand that the relationships that they discover depend on a scale factor.

### Task 1—Perimeters and Areas of Similar Figures

*Jim and the Beanstalk* (Briggs 1997) is a good resource to use to introduce this task. The illustrations show giant-sized eyeglasses and dentures and a huge wig, each of which Jim carries up the bean stalk. You can use the illustrations to ask questions—for example, "How would the area of a lens in eyeglasses for the giant compare with the area of a lens in glasses for Jim? Or glasses for you?"

Give each student a copy of the activity sheet "Scale It Up, Scale It Down" and a copy of "Perimeters and Areas of Similar Figures." Step 1 on "Perimeters and Areas of Similar Figures" presents a table, shown in figure 28, which gives the students scale factors to use in drawing geometric figures that are similar to one that appear on "Scale It Up, Scale It Down" (see the margin). All the sides of those shapes are horizontal or vertical line segments on dot grids. As a result, the perimeters and areas are easy to determine. The restriction on the sides also facilitates students' discoveries of the patterns that allow them to generalize the relationships between the similar figures in each pair.

**Measurements of Preimages and Images**

| Figure | Scale Factor | Length of Longest Side in Preimage (linear units) | Length of Corresponding Side in Image (linear units) | Perimeter of Preimage (linear units) | Perimeter of Image (linear units) | Area of Preimage (square units) | Area of Image (ssquare units) |
|---|---|---|---|---|---|---|---|
| A | 2 | | | | | | |
| B | 3 | | | | | | |
| C | 4 | | | | | | |
| D | $\frac{1}{2}$ | | | | | | |
| E | 2 | | | | | | |
| F | $\frac{3}{2}$ | | | | | | |

Fig. 28.

Students construct dilations for figures A–F according to given scale factors and complete the table.

To construct a figure that is similar to a given figure, the students must measure the length of each side of the preimage and multiply it by the given scale factor to determine the length of the corresponding side of the image. You may need to remind the students that the linear unit of measurement in this task is the horizontal or vertical distance between two dots. Some students may erroneously count the number of dots rather than the number of unit segments between the dots. Remind them, too, that all angles remain the same; that is, corresponding angles of similar figures are congruent. Be alert also to the possibility that some students may mistakenly attempt to add the scale factor to the length of each side. Students can place the scaled image wherever it will fit on the dot grid; in some instances, the preimage and the image may overlap. The students should plan the placement of each image carefully to ensure that it will fit completely on the grid shown.

Figures A–D on "Scale It Up, Scale It Down" are rectangles. Figures E and F are L-shaped and thus are more likely to cause students problems in constructing appropriate similar figures. Creating figure F may involve an additional difficulty because students must multiply the lengths of the sides of the preimage by a fraction. However, all the scale factors, including the fractions, are familiar multipliers. Encourage the students to do the necessary computations mentally.

After the students have succeeded in drawing the similar figures, step 1 continues, directing them to complete the table by determining the

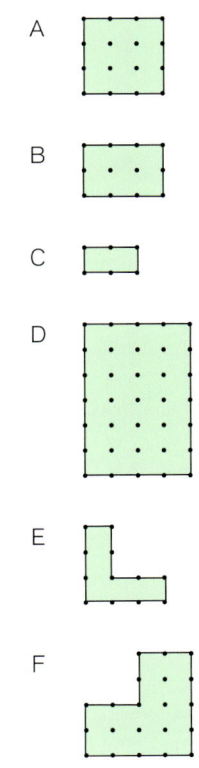

Scale Factors and Measurement Relationships

length of the longest side, the perimeter, and the area for each preimage and image. Finding the longest side will present no difficulty, and most students will probably find the perimeters and areas of both the preimages and the images easily, since the calculations involve concepts that they have explored in the elementary grades. Students may count the number of unit squares inside a figure to find its area, or, for figures A–D, they may apply an area formula for rectangles.

Students are likely to apply different strategies to find the perimeters and areas of figures E and F. Some will simply count the unit segments along the edges of a figure to find its perimeter. Others may extend one or more of the segments to generate a rectangle and then apply a perimeter formula for rectangles. Urge students who use this approach to explain why it yields the correct value.

To determine the areas of figures E and F, students might count the number of unit squares in the interior of each figure, or they might partition the figure into two rectangles, apply an appropriate area formula, and add the results. Another approach is to extend two sides to change the figure into a rectangle and then apply an area formula for a rectangle. However, students who use this approach sometimes neglect to subtract the area of the extension that they added to the preimage or image to create the rectangle.

After the students have constructed the appropriate similar figures and completed the table on the activity sheet, discuss their results before allowing them to proceed to step 2. Let the discussion serve as an opportunity to rectify any errors that the students may have made in constructing an image or calculating a measurement. If you wish, you can project a transparency image of "Scale It Up, Scale It Down" and invite students to draw their solutions on it and share their strategies. Examining the various methods that the students have used to find the perimeters and areas of the figures can be fruitful for the students while allowing you to gain valuable insights into their thinking. Using a transparency of the preimages and images also facilitates the discussion of the lengths of the corresponding sides of the similar figures—particularly in the cases of the more complicated figures, E and F.

In steps 2–4, the students compare each image and preimage with respect to three measurements: the length of the longest side (in step 2), the perimeter (in step 3), and the area (in step 4). They express each comparison as a ratio of a particular measurement in the image to the corresponding measurement in the preimage. As the students review their entries in the table and determine the appropriate ratios in these steps, they should realize (1) that the ratio of the lengths of the corresponding sides of similar figures is the same as the scale factor, (2) that the ratio of the perimeters is also the scale factor, and (3) that the ratio of the areas is the square of the scale factor.

Step 5 asks the students about these patterns. You will probably need to remind some students that for a scale factor of $n$, $n^2$ means $n \times n$ and not $n \times 2$. Depending on their prior experiences with variables, the students may be able to write the relationships symbolically; otherwise, an accurate verbal description of the relationship is acceptable at this grade level.

Step 5(*b*) is designed to determine whether students understand the implications of the conclusions that they have reached in this task. They

*Students should be able to investigate patterns and generalize their observations.*

suppose that they are going to enlarge a geometric figure that has a perimeter of 13 units and an area of 16 square units by a scale factor of 250 percent. Although most students will be able to determine that the enlarged figure will have a perimeter of 13 × 2.5, or 32.5, units, some students may mistakenly compute the area of the image to be 16 × 2.5 rather than 16 × (2.5)². In other words, they are likely to neglect to square the scale factor before they multiply it by the area of the original figure.

Step 6 is optional for students who have worked with the area formula for a circle. It poses a problem about the relationship between similar figures in an everyday context. If a pizzeria prices its pizzas by the unit of area and charges $5 for a small pizza that is 6 inches in diameter, how much should the pizzeria charge for a new pizza that is 12 inches in diameter? Some students may erroneously assume that the cost of the larger pizza should be twice the cost of the smaller pizza. However, the large pizza is the image of the small pizza with a scale factor of 2. Thus, the area of the large pizza has 2², or 4, times the area of the small pizza and should cost $5 × 4, or $20. (Students who apply the formula for the area of a circle can see that the area of the small pizza, which has a radius of 3 inches, is π(3)², or 9π square inches, and the area of the large pizza, which has a radius of 6 inches, is π(6)², or 36π square inches. Thus, the area of the large pizza is four times that of the small one.) For various economic and business reasons, however, the cost of a large pizza is often less than four times the cost of a smaller pizza with half the diameter.

### Task 2—Surface Areas and Volumes of Similar Figures

The second task extends the ideas developed in the first one to three-dimensional geometric figures. Give each student a copy of the activity sheet "Surface Areas and Volumes of Similar Figures," and provide each group of students with 150 centimeter cubes (or other small cubes) and a calculator. In step 1, the students use the cubes to build each rectangular prism, A–E, whose dimensions are specified in the table (see fig. 29).

**Measurements of Preimages and Images**

| Figure (Preimage) | Dimensions of Preimage (centimeters) | Scale Factor | Surface Area of Preimage (square centimeters) | Surface Area of Image (square centimeters) | Volume of Preimage (cubic centimeters) | Volume of Image (cubic centimeters) |
|---|---|---|---|---|---|---|
| A | 1 × 2 × 3 | 2 | | | | |
| B | 1 × 2 × 1 | 3 | | | | |
| C | 1 × 1 × 1 | 4 | | | | |
| D | 2 × 2 × 4 | $\frac{1}{2}$ | | | | |
| E | 4 × 2 × 4 | $\frac{3}{2}$ | | | | |

Fig. 29.

Students construct dilations for figures A–E according to given scale factors and complete the table.

*Making a scale model helps students put comparisons in perspective.*

This time, though, the students should complete the table one row at a time, since building all the preimages and images at once would take more cubes than they have. Working together, they should build figure A and its image and then determine and record the surface areas and volumes of the two similar figures. After completing row 1, they should move on to row 2, building figure B and its image, and so on.

The concrete models make it easy for students to compute the surface areas and volumes of the prisms. Each face of the centimeter cube has a surface area of one square centimeter; the volume of each cube is one cubic centimeter. Thus, students can determine the surface areas and volumes of the figures that they construct by counting square centimeters or cubic centimeters.

In steps 2 and 3, the students compare each image and preimage with respect to two measurements—surface area and volume. They express each comparison as a ratio of a measurement in the image to the corresponding measurement in the preimage, and they describe patterns that they observe. The experience of building the prisms instead of simply applying formulas for the surface areas and volumes can be powerful. Applying a scale factor to a preimage and actually observing the changes in the measurements of the image can help students see that the ratio of the surface area of the image to the surface area of the preimage is the square of the scale factor and that the ratio of the volume of the image to the volume of the preimage is the cube of the scale factor. In step 4, the students offer their conclusions.

Students should recognize that the relationship between the surface areas of similar three-dimensional figures is exactly the same as the relationship between the areas of similar two-dimensional figures. Depending on your students' prior experiences, they may be able to understand and explain why the area ratios are the same for figures in both two and three dimensions. Help them realize that area is a two-dimensional measurement, even in a three-dimensional figure. Because an image multiplies the length of each side or edge of a preimage by the scale factor, the area of the image multiplies that of a preimage by the scale factor in both the horizontal and the vertical dimensions. The result is the same as multiplying the area of the preimage by the square of the scale factor. Likewise, the volume of the image of a prism multiples the length, width, and height of the preimage by the scale factor. In other words, the volume of the image multiples that of the preimage by the scale factor in each of the three dimensions. The result is the same as multiplying the volume of the preimage by the cube of the scale factor.

Step 5 asks the students to suppose that a building has a volume of 100,000 cubic feet and they must build a scale model by using a scale factor of $\frac{1}{100}$. What will the volume of the model be? ($\frac{1}{10}$ cubic foot) Use your students' work on this problem to assess their ability to apply the relationship between the volumes of similar figures in an everyday context. They should be able to compute the volume of the model by multiplying the volume of the building by the cube of the scale factor.

### Task 3—Scale Models

In the final task of this investigation, students use ratios to reason about scale factors. Give each student a copy of the activity sheet "Scale Models," and let the students work independently or in groups.

Maps and other models often display conversions that involve two different units of measurement; for example, for HO model trains, 1 inch represents 7.25 feet, and on some maps, 1 inch represents 25 miles. Although these conversion factors enable us to make sense of the size of the model train or the distances on a map, they are not scale factors. Scale factors are ratios, so they are comparisons between two quantities expressed in the same unit of measurement. To generate a ratio from the information in a conversion, students must express both quantities in the same unit. To do so, they must use knowledge from previous measurement experiences to convert one of the measures. For instance, suppose that they read that 1 inch represents 10 miles on a map. Using measurement facts—1 mile = 5280 feet and 1 foot = 12 inches—they can convert the information:

$$\frac{1 \text{ inch}}{10 \text{ miles}} = \frac{1 \text{ inch}}{10 \times 5280 \text{ feet}} = \frac{1 \text{ inch}}{52{,}800 \text{ feet}} = \frac{1 \text{ inch}}{52{,}800 \times 12 \text{ inches}} = \frac{1 \text{ inch}}{633{,}600 \text{ inches}}.$$

So the scale factor between the distance on the map and the actual distance is

$$\frac{1}{633{,}600}.$$

In other words, the actual distance is 633,600 times the distance on the map. Steps 1 and 2 on the activity sheet "Scale Models" present problems of this type.

In step 3, the students move beyond a simple determination of a scale factor to using a scale factor to make comparisons of areas. A language arts context—the fictional world of Jonathan Swift's classic, *Gulliver's Travels*—supplies the context for a three-part problem. The students suppose that Gulliver is 6 feet tall and the Lilliputians are 6 inches high—exact measurements given in two contemporary adaptations of the story for younger readers: *Gulliver's Adventures in Lilliput* (Beneduce 1996) and *Gulliver in Lilliput* (Hodges 1995). In part (*a*), the students compare a Lilliputian's height to Gulliver's by converting feet to inches to discover the linear scale factor between Gulliver and a Lilliputian: 6 feet = 72 inches, so the scale factor is

$$\frac{72 \text{ inches}}{6 \text{ inches}}, \text{ or } \frac{12}{1}.$$

All linear measurements of Gulliver would be in this ratio to corresponding linear measurements of the Lilliputian. For example, the students would expect Gulliver's arms to be 12 times as long as the arms of the Lilliputian.

Moreover, on the basis of their earlier work with the areas of similar figures, the students would expect all measurements of area for Gulliver—the area of his forehead, for example—to be $12^2$, or 144, times corresponding area measurements for a Lilliputian. Thus, students should be able to solve the problem presented in part (*b*), which asks them to imagine a mattress on which Gulliver could sleep comfortably and a mattress on which a Lilliputian could sleep with equal comfort. Then they determine possible dimensions for the surfaces of the two similar mattresses.

Part (*c*) moves the students to a comparison of volumes of rooms suitable for Gulliver and a Lilliputian. The volume of Gulliver's living

*Maps and other models often display conversions that involve two different units of measurement.*

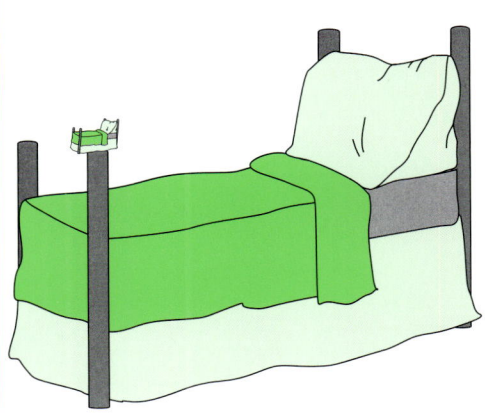

Scale Factors and Measurement Relationships

*Literature that involves mathematical ideas appeals to middle-grades students and can be a springboard for exploring ratios and proportions.*

For related activities, see "Exploring Proportional Reasoning through Movies and Literature" (Beckmann, Thompson, and Austin 2004) and "Locusts for Lunch: Connecting Mathematics, Science, and Literature" (Austin, Thompson, and Beckmann 2006). Both articles are available on the CD-ROM.

room would be $12^3$, or 1728, times the volume of a comparable Lilliputian living room.

Step 4 gives the students greater scope for invention as they continue to experiment with the impact of a scale factor on the size of an image. Give each student one or two sheets of quarter-inch grid paper for the work. This time, they create preimages, select scale factors, and produce images on their own. To introduce this step, you might read aloud the children's book *Cut Down to Size at High Noon* (Sundby 2000). The story presents the western town of Cowlick, where the barber and a newly arrived competitor scale objects of local significance (a grasshopper, a train engine) up or down in hairstyles that present perfectly proportioned images of them.

You can use the story and its colorful illustrations to capture the students' attention and then lead a discussion of how the barbers create the scaled designs to prepare the students for their work with scale drawings in step 4. Encourage them to be creative as they draw a person, object, or abstract design. Then they must choose a scale factor, use it to make an image—either an enlargement or a reduction—of the drawing, and compare the areas of the drawing and its image.

### Extensions

In this investigation, students explore various relationships between images and their preimages whose dimensions are multiplied by the same scale factor, resulting in the similar figures. If you judge that your students are ready for more advanced work, you can ask them to apply different scale factors to the horizontal and the vertical dimensions of a two-dimensional figure and determine how the area of the resulting image compares with that of the preimage. They should find that the area of the image is the product of the area of the preimage and the horizontal and vertical scale factors.

For an even greater challenge, the students can apply different scale factors to each of the dimensions of three-dimensional figures and explore the relationship between the volume of each preimage and that of its image. The students should discover that the volume of each resulting image is the product of the volume of the preimage and the three scale factors.

## Assessment

Assessment should be an ongoing process throughout the investigation as you observe your students as they build similar figures with given scale factors; find perimeters, areas, and volumes of preimages and images; and generalize the patterns that they observe. Their work in step 6 on the activity sheet "Perimeters and Areas of Similar Figures," step 5 on "Surface Areas and Volumes of Similar Figures," and step 4 on "Scale Models" will give you an opportunity to assess their ability to apply the relationships between corresponding perimeters, areas, and volumes of similar figures to solve problems.

## Reflections

Middle-grades students have found this investigation engaging—particularly when their teachers have introduced the tasks with stories.

As students investigate the relationships among the corresponding perimeters, areas, and volumes of similar figures, they should reason about the patterns that they observe and attempt to generalize their observations in appropriate conjectures. Students need opportunities to explore such patterns and speculate about relationships on their own, with help from you in refining their statements of their ideas.

Consider using this investigation in conjunction with the algebra investigation, Block Buildings, for an extended exploration that will incorporate algebra, geometry, and measurement concepts with the making of conjectures about relationships. Using tasks that integrate content strands is one means of maximizing the benefits of instruction in the limited time that teachers have for mathematics. In addition, tasks that integrate multiple strands help students realize that they can apply a single concept in different contexts.

*Tasks that integrate multiple strands help students realize that they can apply a single concept in different contexts.*

## Connections

This investigation incorporates concepts from several content strands, including measurement, geometry (similar figures), algebra (pattern generalization), and number and operations (ratios). In addition, the tasks in the investigation lay the foundation for increasingly formal work with similarity in high school geometry and with concepts of variation in second-year algebra. For example, in geometry, students study fundamental relationships of similarity. Two similar figures with a scale factor of $k$ have—

- corresponding angles that are congruent;
- corresponding lengths and perimeters that are in a ratio of $k$;
- corresponding areas that are in a ratio of $k^2$; and
- corresponding volumes that are in a ratio of $k^3$.

In second-year algebra, students often study fundamental properties of variation. If $y$ varies directly as $x^n$, and $x$ is multiplied by $k$, then $y$ is multiplied by $k^n$; if $y$ varies inversely as $x^n$, and $x$ is multiplied by $k \neq 0$, then $y$ is divided by $k^n$. Investigating these relationships with concrete materials in the middle grades gives students a good preparation for studying the same concepts more abstractly in high school.

Task 3 (Scale Models) specifically connects ideas of scale to familiar objects in the everyday world. The students' work with conversions and scales relates to map skills in social studies. Connections to literature help students see that scale factors are often the basis of stories—even ones that do not explicitly discuss scale factors. Likewise, scale factors are evident in movies that feature people or objects of different sizes, such as the popular Lord of the Rings or Harry Potter series. Your students might enjoy considering how filmmakers use the mathematics of scale in such movies.

> *"Well-chosen problems can be particularly valuable in developing or deepening students' understanding of important mathematical ideas."*
> *(NCTM 2000, p. 256)*

# Fitness Fest

## Focus

Reasoning about data relationships

## Overview

In this investigation, students summarize data and create and apply rules to sets of data to make decisions. The context is a schoolwide fitness festival, Fitness Field Day, which includes running and jumping contests. The students enter into this context vicariously, by reading a newspaper-style account of the fitness festival at the fictitious school that provides the setting for the problem—Washington Elementary and Junior High School. After responding to "readiness" questions that probe their understanding of the context and their ability to interpret data from a table, the students encounter the problem. Working in small groups, they must divide the sixth-grade festival participants into three teams that are roughly comparable in ability. The data on each participant include two running scores, one jumping score, and a mark of "pass" or "fail" on a fitness test. A successful solution to the problem involves not only developing an effective data analysis procedure for dividing the participants into competitive teams but also generalizing the method for use in forming other such teams in similar situations. Each group of problem solvers prepares a presentation to the festival's organizers (played by the students in the other groups), explaining its method step by step and permitting the organizers to test it by applying it to data on the seventh-grade participants. In addition, the festival's organizers hope to identify a method that all the schools in the district can use in their fitness festivals. Thus, on the basis of the results of the evaluation of its work, each group refines its method and submits a letter outlining its revised procedure to the coordinator of the organizing committee (the teacher).

## Goals

- Develop a data-analysis procedure for making decisions on the basis of categorical and numerical data
- Explain a statistical methodology in a presentation to the class and a revised methodology to the teacher in a letter
- Analyze and evaluate the statistical methodologies of peers and offer suggestions for improvements in the methodology

## Mathematical Content

This investigation supports the following Content and Process Standards and expectations for grades 6–8 (NCTM 2000, pp. 399, 401–2):

---

The development of this activity was supported by the School Mathematics and Science Center (SMSC), Purdue University, West Lafayette, Indiana, under the direction of Richard Lesh.

# Data Analysis and Probability

- Select and use appropriate statistical methods to analyze data
- Develop and evaluate inferences and predictions that are based on data

*Measurement*

- Understand measurable attributes of objects and the units, systems, and processes of measurement

*Problem Solving*

- Build new mathematical knowledge through problem solving
- Solve problems that arise in mathematics and in other contexts
- Apply and adapt a variety of appropriate strategies to solve problems

*Reasoning and Proof*

- Make and investigate mathematical conjectures
- Develop and evaluate mathematical arguments and proofs
- Select and use various types of reasoning and methods of proof

*Communication*

- Communicate … mathematical thinking coherently and clearly to peers, teachers, and others

*Connections*

- Recognize and apply mathematics in contexts outside of mathematics

In this investigation, students develop concepts of data analysis and statistical modeling that they will need for making decisions based on data sets in both everyday and workplace situations. Filtering and selecting data are important skills that the investigation introduces. For example, students might decide to use all the available data—running, jumping, and fitness scores—to assign participants to teams, reasoning that the three scores together provide an overall profile of an athlete. Alternatively, they might filter out the fitness score, arguing that only the running and jumping scores apply in the track-and-field events. Another statistical skill that students might use in developing their methodology is stochastic processing, which involves determining the ranking order of data on the basis of one criterion and then modifying the order on the basis of a secondary criterion. Students might employ a rudimentary version of this technique by initially ranking participants on the basis of their jumping scores and then modifying the order on the basis of the two running scores.

Another important mathematical idea that students encounter in Fitness Fest is generalization. They are required not only to assign the sixth-grade students to teams but also to develop and describe a generalizable data-analysis procedure that could be used to assign seventh graders to teams. This form of generalization hones students' reasoning, problem-solving, and communication skills.

Developing data-driven decision-making procedures is foundational to creating mathematical models, including computer-based models for predicting weather.

pp. 95, 96, 97–98, 99

## Prior Knowledge or Experience

- Experience in interpreting whole-unit measurements of time and length (e.g., seconds, minutes, and inches)
- Experience in reading and interpreting simple tables
- Work in comparing and ordering measurements with decimal units and mixed units (for example, feet and inches)
- Facility with basic number operations (using either a calculator or paper and pencil)

## Materials

For each student—
- A copy of each of the following activity sheets:
  - "Fun on the Field"
  - "Fielding the Facts"
  - "Fitness Fest Investigation"
  - "Seventh-Grade Performance Data"
- Paper and pencil
- A calculator (optional)

For each group of students—
- Overhead transparencies and transparency pens
- Access to computers with word processing and spreadsheet software (optional)

For the teacher—
- An overhead projector

## Classroom Environment

Students work independently to read "Fun on the Field" and answer questions about it on "Fielding the Facts." After this preparation, they work in groups of three at clustered desks or tables to develop a data analysis procedure to solve the problem on "Fitness Fest Investigation." Each group then presents its work, with the students in the other groups evaluating the proposed method by applying it to the information on "Seventh-Grade Performance Data." The groups' presentations to the class and their subsequent revisions to their procedures are important means of formative assessment.

## Investigation

To set the stage for this investigation, give each student a copy of the activity sheet "Fun on the Field," which presents a newspaper-style account of an all-school fitness festival. Reading this piece will familiarize the students with the context of the investigation. Also provide each student with a copy of the activity sheet "Fielding the Facts," which poses questions on the account and presents data in a table as a way of reviewing the important skill of reading information displayed in this manner.

Use the students' responses as a basis for discussing Fitness Field Day and the data in the table. Call the students' attention to question 4, which asks why the organizers of Fitness Field Day want to ensure that

*Students "should expand the audience for their mathematical arguments beyond their teacher and their classmates. They need to develop compelling arguments with enough evidence to convince someone who is not part of their own learning community."*

*(NCTM 2000, p. 262)*

all the teams are approximately equal in ability. Emphasize that the organizers want all the teams to be competitive. The goal of creating a fair competition can motivate the students in the investigation. Be sure that they interpret the data in the table correctly, recognizing that in some events, such as the high jump, a high score is desirable, but in other events, such as the 800-meter run, a low score is best. This distinction is important in ranking the athletes correctly.

Assign the students to groups of three. Give each student a copy of the activity sheet "Fitness Fest Investigation," which sets the scene:

*The situation:* Washington Elementary and Junior High School will soon hold its annual Fitness Field Day. However, the organizers of the festival still must assign the sixth- and seventh-grade athletes to teams for the track and field events. The organizers want to be sure that all the teams entering these events are roughly equal in ability. They have collected data on the performances of each track and field athlete in the sixth and seventh grades.

A table on the activity sheet shows data on the sixth-grade athletes (see fig. 29).

Next, the students encounter a statement of the problem:

*The problem:* Help the organizers with their work. Use their data to develop a method for assigning the sixth-grade participants to three teams that you would expect to be roughly equal in ability. Work on this problem with the other members of your group.

### Sixth Graders' Fitness Scores

| Student | 100-Meter Run | 800-Meter Run | High Jump | Fitness Test* |
|---|---|---|---|---|
| Betsy | 17.3 sec | 3 min 38 sec | 5'3" | Pass |
| Caroline | 16.0 sec | 3 min 1 sec | 3'5" | Fail |
| Daniel | 19.89 sec | 2 min 42 sec | 5'5" | Pass |
| Dick | 18.52 sec | 2 min 55 sec | 4'4" | Pass |
| Jason | 16.48 sec | 2 min 55 sec | 3'9" | Pass |
| Judi | 17.2 sec | 3 min 22 sec | 3'6" | Fail |
| Linda | 20.2 sec | 4 min 0 sec | 5'0" | Pass |
| Mack | 18.25 sec | 3 min 16 sec | 5'6" | Pass |
| Manuel | 17.1 sec | 3 min 11 sec | 4'2" | Fail |
| Margret | 20.32 sec | 2 min 51 sec | 5'7" | Pass |
| Michelle | 16.44 sec | 2 min 45 sec | 4'5" | Fail |
| Rob | 19.2 sec | 3 min 12 sec | 4'10" | Fail |
| Sandra | 17.34 sec | 3 min 50 sec | 5'1" | Fail |
| Scott | 17.0 sec | 3 min 30 sec | 4'11" | Pass |
| Susan | 18.3 sec | 3 min 0 sec | 5'3" | Pass |

*All students received a mark of "pass" or "fail." The test consisted of 30 push-ups, 50 jumping jacks, and 20 sit-ups.

**Fig. 29.**

The organizers of Fitness Field Day provide a table displaying data on the athletic performances of the sixth graders.

Read the statements of the situation and the problem aloud, or call on a student to read them. To be sure that everyone understands the task, ask the students to describe what they must produce. Be certain that they know that each group must come up with three equitable sixth-grade teams, and to do this, the group must first develop a method of analyzing the data on the sixth-grade participants.

This is not all that the students need to do, however. In addition, each group must present its results and its method, giving an explanation that is so clear that others can use it on another data set. The next section of the sheet explains this part of the task:

> ***What's next?*** When all the groups have developed their methods, each one will present its teams and give a step-by-step explanation of its procedure for determining them. As each group makes its presentation, the members of all the other groups will play the parts of the organizers of Fitness Field Day. They will ask questions, and then they will evaluate the method by testing it on new data. They will have data on the seventh-grade participants in Fitness Field Day, and they will use the method to assign these participants to teams.

Explain that each group will organize its work on transparencies for a presentation on the overhead projector. Emphasize that each group should be ready for probing questions and detailed comments on its procedure.

When all the groups' methods have been critiqued, each group must review its method and make any necessary improvements, because the organizers of the festival have big plans for an effective method:

> ***The impact:*** After all the groups have made their presentations, each one will revise and improve its method. The organizers of Fitness Field Day hope to identify an effective method that they can recommend to all the schools in the district for use in all the annual field day competitions. When your group has finalized its method, all the team members should work together to write a letter to the coordinator of the organizing committee—your teacher—explaining the group's procedure and highlighting its advantages.

If your students have access to computers with word-processing software, allow them to use it in composing their letters.

This investigation requires reasoning and problem-solving processes that are essential for real-world mathematical modeling to make predictions or decisions. Successful group work in an investigation of this sort typically leads students through cycles of developing, testing, and revising trial procedures. In the early stages, the students devise simplistic definitions and rules that their groups then test, debate, and revise.

For example, one group of students began work by finding the average score for each competition. As the group calculated the averages, one of the students said that she didn't see how these averages would help them divide the participants into teams. This comment led the students to rethink their approach and realize that they needed to find an average, or summary, for each participant rather than for each contest.

The students started to add the three scores for each participant and then divide that sum by 3, but this time they noticed a different problem: although high scores are desirable in the high jump, low

*Providing a challenging investigation to small groups of students facilitates reasoning, argument, and assessment throughout the problem-solving process.*

scores are best in running events, so adding the data does not make sense. This realization led the group to explore a system that assigned an ordered rank to each participant for each contest. The students then added the three ordered ranks for each athlete and divided the sum by 3 to produce an "average ordered rank" for each participant. The opportunity for students to test their trial procedures and revise them on the basis of the results is similar to the design process used by engineers, architects, and workers in other fields that are heavily dependent on mathematics.

Another group also went through design cycles as it improved its procedure for assigning participants to teams. The students initially ranked the athletes from first to twelfth on the basis of their performances in each event. They then added the ranks for each participant and ordered the participants according to the sum of the ranks. Next, they used the sum to assign the highest-ranked athlete to team 1, the second-ranked participant to team 2, and so forth, as follows:

| Team 1 | Team 2 | Team 3 |
| --- | --- | --- |
| 1st ranked | 2nd ranked | 3rd ranked |
| 4th ranked | 5th ranked | 6th ranked |
| 7th ranked | 8th ranked | 9th ranked |
| 10th ranked | 11th ranked | 12th ranked |
| 13th ranked | 14th ranked | 15th ranked |

After starting this process, one of the students in the group said, "Wait! Team 1 is always going to be the best team because on each round they get the best of the next three!" This insight resulted in the following revision of the procedure:

| Team 1 | Team 2 | Team 3 |
| --- | --- | --- |
| 1st ranked | 2nd ranked | 3rd ranked |
| 6th ranked | 5th ranked | 4th ranked |
| 7th ranked | 8th ranked | 9th ranked |
| 12th ranked | 11th ranked | 10th ranked |
| 13th ranked | 14th ranked | 15th ranked |

The sample solutions below illustrate different procedures for assigning participants to competitive teams. Each solution represents work that students revised after presenting their method to the class and receiving feedback from other students, as well as the teacher's comments on the group's solution in a letter. Each method has particular strengths and weaknesses.

### Sample Solution 1

1. For each event, rank the participants from first to fifteenth place.
2. Add the ranks for each participant to obtain a total score. For example, Betsy was seventh in the 100-meter race, thirteenth in the 800-meter race, and tied for fourth place in the high jump (she was assigned a rank of 4.5). Therefore, her total score was 24.5.

> Students' thinking is revealed by their dialogue when they are working on challenging problems in small groups. Such situations offer teachers excellent opportunities to assess students' reasoning.

3. Put the participants in order from the lowest total score (overall, the best ranking) to the highest score (overall, the worst ranking).
4. Put the participants into groups of three (the top three scores, the next three scores, and so on) until five groups have been created.
5. Assign one participant from each group to one of the three teams so that each team has a member from each of the five groups.
6. Make adjustments to create teams with approximately equal total scores (for example, team 1, 119.5: team 2, 120.5: team 3, 120.0). Make additional adjustments to assign to the teams equal numbers of members who passed and failed the fitness test.

This procedure resulted in the following teams:

Team 1: Michelle, Jason, Mack, Sandra, Linda

Team 2: Daniel, Caroline, Scott, Dick, Rob

Team 3: Margret, Susan, Betsy, Manuel, Judi

Sample solution 1 illustrates a procedure that begins by summarizing the three performance ranks for each participant. The method then uses the summary score to develop an overall rank order for the students. By distributing participants and checking for the overall equivalence of the teams' scores—thus allowing for adjustments where necessary—the method offers an effective way of forming equivalent teams.

Note, however, that after giving each athlete a summary score on his or her performances, this method pays no further attention to individual performances on particular events as it assigns students to teams. As a result, it allows the formation of a team that has little hope of winning a particular event. The statement of the problem does not specifically require that the teams have nearly equal probabilities of winning an event. Sometimes problems can be interpreted in different ways. Students should realize that solving a problem sometimes requires a restatement of the problem to make it sufficiently specific to produce a satisfactory solution while avoiding unintended results. An evaluation of the method in sample solution 1 indicates that the students could improve the last step by making the procedure for modifying the team membership more specific.

**Sample Solution 2**

1. For each contest, rank the participants from first to fifteenth place.
2. Put the top performer in each contest on a separate team. For example, Caroline is first in the 100-meter run, Daniel is first in the 800-meter run, and Margret is first in the high jump, so each is assigned to a different team.
3. Distribute the remaining students among the teams as fairly as possible, with the students having the second best records in each event distributed among the teams, and the students having the third best records in each event distributed among the teams, and so on.

This procedure produced the following teams:
  Team 1: Caroline, Mack, Dick, Judi, Linda
  Team 2: Daniel, Michelle, Betsy, Manuel, Scott
  Team 3: Margret, Jason, Susan, Sandra, Rob

Sample solution 2 uses the actual performance of participants on individual events to assign participants to teams, rather than a summary score, as in sample solution 1. The intention is to ensure that each team has a possibility of winning in each of the running and jumping contests. However, an evaluation of this solution indicates that the third step is not specified well enough to produce reliable results. In other words, if two different people applied the procedure, they would not necessarily produce teams made up of the same participants. The students could greatly improve the method by stating the third step in more detail.

*Extensions*

Fitness Fest opens the door to further work in data analysis. Follow-up activities can help students develop their data-analysis procedures and decision-making capabilities:

- Each group can apply the data-analysis procedures in the sample solutions on the CD-ROM to the information from "Seventh-Grade Performance Data." The application of various procedures gives students practice in various skills while they test the procedures and make suggestions for improving them.

- Students can enter the data from either the sixth-grade or the seventh-grade data set into a spreadsheet and then use the spreadsheet software to implement the various procedures presented in class and in the sample solutions.

- Students can plan their own Fitness Fest, gathering data from events in their physical education classes and then using the procedures that they have already developed to form equitable teams. This activity allows students to adapt their procedures to larger sets of participants, different events, and different numbers of teams.

- Students can create a procedure for judging events and combining scores. Relevant questions include the following: Do all members of the team participate in each event? If not, who will participate in which contest? If multiple team members participate in each event, how will the team be scored?

## Assessment

The groups' presentations of their methods offer rich opportunities for peer- and self-assessment. When the presenters' peers apply the proposed procedure to the data for the seventh-grade participants, they naturally begin to pose questions and make suggestions about the clarity, completeness, and effectiveness of the approach. Their feedback enables the presenters to revise their product.

The investigation integrates your assessment completely in the scenario. Acting as the Fitness Field Day coordinator, you can assess the groups' final products in letters to them. In each letter, indicate what is useful about the solution and what needs clarification or improvement.

Students' work on the seventh-grade data set through approaches similar to the two described here can be found on the CD-ROM. See "Fitness Fest: Sample Student Work on the Seventh-Grade Data Set."

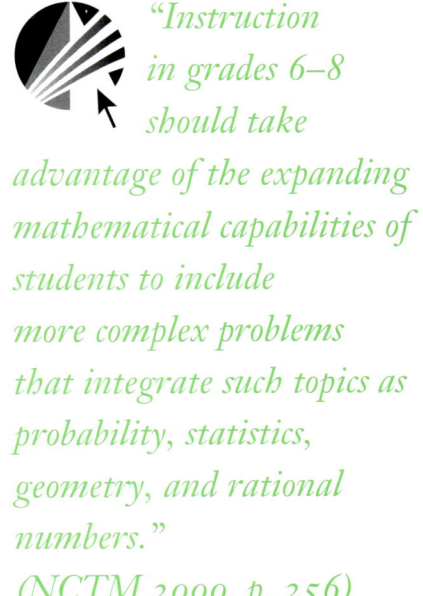

*"Instruction in grades 6–8 should take advantage of the expanding mathematical capabilities of students to include more complex problems that integrate such topics as probability, statistics, geometry, and rational numbers."*
(NCTM 2000, p. 256)

*"Mathematics involves ... making conjectures about possible generalizations and evaluating the conjectures."*
(NCTM 2000, p. 262)

*"An important aspect of a problem-solving orientation toward mathematics is making and examining conjectures raised by solving a problem and posing follow-up questions."*
(NCTM 2000, p. 261)

Pose questions that prompt your students to question certain aspects of their procedure. To lend an air of authenticity to the experience, you might ask coordinators of competitive events in the community to donate their time to observe and respond to the presentations, writing letters of their own to the students.

To encourage self-assessment, you might enlarge the sample solutions on the CD-ROM, make transparencies of them, and have the class study the solutions and compose letters offering critiques of them. Alternatively, you and your students could decide together what criteria to use to "grade" the sample solutions. Students could then use these grading guidelines to revise their own work, or you could use them to assign a grade to the final products.

Many students need to complete a few of these types of investigations and engage in shared assessment experiences to learn what constitutes good work. Consequently, some teachers grade early investigations on the basis of completeness and full participation and reserve more stringent criteria for later work from students.

## Reflections

The students' work in Fitness Fest represents thinking and reasoning processes that are necessary for making real-world decisions based on data analysis. Successful solutions involve formulating the problem clearly—a step that includes explicitly stating assumptions about how to process data to form teams. Problem solvers almost always go through cycles of developing, testing, and revising trial approaches before arriving at a successful solution. As students engage in such cycles of interpretation and reinterpretation, they are likely to move beyond simple numerical computations toward holistic sense making that will enable them to develop sophisticated solutions.

Although interactions with peers and cycles of revision usually lead to improved procedures, students often exhibit misconceptions of two types in this investigation. A lack of familiarity with complex problems characterizes one type, and misunderstandings about the context of the investigation characterize the other. A few examples of both types of misconceptions follow:

- Students may think that they need to identify exactly one correct approach and apply one particular procedure that the teacher has in mind. They may become frustrated or even resist engaging in the problem because they think that the teacher has not presented a well-formulated, or "good," problem. They also may feel at a loss, thinking that developing an approach to such a problem is overwhelming. To help students overcome these reactions, explain to them explicitly that they can develop several good procedures to reach the goals of the investigation and that real-world problems often have a number of good solutions.

- Students may expect to identify and use a mathematical or statistical procedure that they have previously learned. Mathematical problem solving in everyday life often involves proposing solutions and refining them through cycles of testing and revising, but students are often surprised when problems in their own mathematics classes call for such a process. Explain that modifying initial ideas is both a process that they should expect to use and a good problem-solving strategy. As students engage in more investigations like these, they will begin to understand that cycles of development and revision of solutions are a natural and desirable part of the problem-solving process.

- When rank ordering the participants on the basis of their performances, students may not understand that a high score (that is, a great height) in the high jump and a low score (that is, a short time) in the 800-meter race both qualify for numerically low (that is, "good") rankings. Although students may recognize this distinction when it is brought to their attention, they still may fail to take it into account when they are immersed in the complexities of the problem-solving process.
- Students may not recognize the impact of variation in individuals' performances. For example, Mack is in the bottom half of the rankings for his performances in the two races, but he placed second in the high jump and passed the fitness test. He could be a valuable asset to a team that needed a good high jumper. Caroline also displays considerable variation in her scores. Although her overall rank is only 7 and she came in last in the high jump and seventh in the 800-meter race, she ranked first in the 100-meter race. Despite having failed the fitness test, she could be a big help to a team by placing well in the 100-meter race. Although students may not immediately recognize the effect of these types of variation, working with data that exhibit them encourages students to move beyond the obvious data to consider other variables.

## Connections

This investigation incorporates connections both with other areas of the curriculum and within mathematics. Within mathematics, students use number sense and arithmetic skills throughout the problem-solving process. They also learn the foundations of exploratory data analysis as they devise and revise procedures, apply them, critique them, and revise them again. The investigation addresses the notion of generalization—an idea that sixth-grade data curricula do not commonly include—by requiring students to produce a procedure that can be applied to new data sets.

Cross-curricular connections in the investigation are primarily with reading and language arts. Reading the newspaper article and responding to the readiness questions would be appropriate activities for reading and language-arts periods. When students prepare for presentations and deliver them, they engage in oral, visual, and written mathematical communication, using skills from both language arts and mathematics.

*Modifying initial ideas is both a process that students should expect to use and oa good problem-solving strategy.*

**NAVIGATIONS SERIES**

**GRADE 6**

# Problem Solving and Reasoning

## Looking Back and Looking Ahead

The investigations in this book emphasize problem solving and reasoning in the content strands of the mathematics curriculum—number and operations, algebra, geometry, measurement, and data analysis and probability. The explorations have been designed to stimulate students to think and reason while solving interesting problems.

Problem solving is the cornerstone of all school mathematics, prekindergarten–grade 12. Concepts and computational skills are not very useful if they are not accompanied by the ability to solve problems. A student who can divide accurately but cannot recognize a situation that calls for division is very limited as a problem solver.

The goal of all school mathematics is to enable all students to use facts, concepts, and procedures to solve increasingly challenging problems as they progress in school. Students in grades 3–6 should have daily experiences with problems that interest them and challenge them to think about various ideas in mathematical contexts. Good problems and problem-solving situations encourage both reasoning and communication. They stimulate students to exchange ideas with one another and with their teachers. These experiences also challenge students to develop and apply strategies, introduce them to new concepts, and provide a context for applying the skills that they have learned.

Teachers can help students become good problem solvers by selecting appropriate problems, giving students time to think and develop solution strategies, encouraging them to discuss their ideas, and assessing their understanding of the mathematics involved. Because good problems are challenging, students may encounter difficulty in arriving at solutions. Teachers must decide when their own input is necessary and when it is not. It is important for teachers and students to realize that challenging problems take time and that perseverance is necessary.

Students in grades 3–6 are poised to make important transitions in their reasoning. Until this time, many students have believed that something is always true if they have seen one or more examples of it. Now students learn that several examples are not sufficient to establish the general truth of a conjecture, and they discover that a single counterexample can show that a conjecture is not true.

Upper elementary students also need to learn what constitutes an acceptable explanation. Teachers must encourage them to explain and justify their thinking and help them learn how to detect fallacies in other students' thinking. Students should also move from considering individual mathematical objects (this triangle) to thinking about classes of objects (all triangles).

The process of problem solving and reasoning is not learned at any particular grade level but unfolds, deepens, and grows each year. As students enter the middle grades, they should have a sound mathematical foundation on which they can build mathematics that is more challenging than anything that they have encountered before.

All mathematics educators aim to teach more mathematics and to teach it better. To do so, they must model good problem-solving strategies and exhibit logical reasoning in the classroom. Students whose teachers are exemplary role models will be positively disposed toward mathematics.

# Navigations Series
## Grade 6

# Problem Solving and Reasoning

## Appendix
### Blackline Masters and Solutions

# Finding Triangular Area

Name_____

1. Use the triangles in your set of pattern blocks to measure the area of the irregular polygon below.

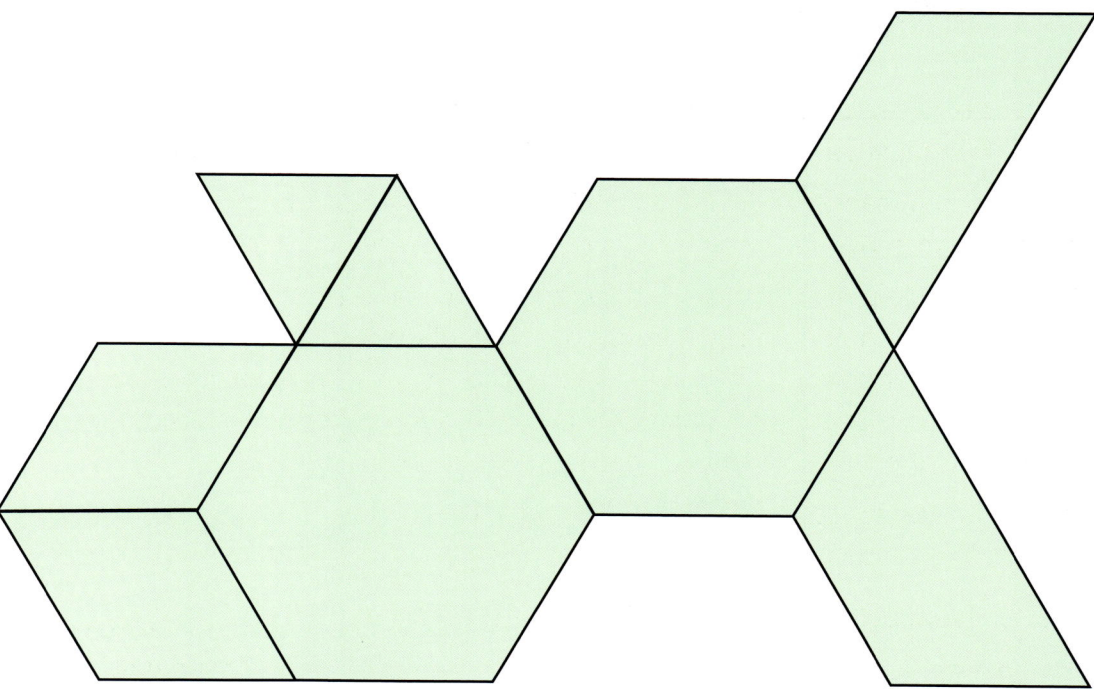

2. The area of the polygon is _____ triangular units.

# Design a Spaceship Panel

Names _____

_____

_____

_____

Your team's mission is to use pattern blocks to design the top panel of a new spaceship. Your panel must be an irregular polygon. It must use at least eight blocks, including at least one of each type (shape) of block.

Your team includes a commander, an engineer, a pilot, and a scientist — each with a special role in the mission. However, all the members are responsible for the team's work.

Each team member should propose a design. Then the commander should lead a discussion of each one. Next, the team should work together to select a design, which the engineer should then inspect to make sure that it shows an irregular polygon. Then the scientist should draw the selected panel accurately on isometric dot paper. Finally, the pilot should use triangles from the set of pattern blocks to measure the area of the panel — and the area of each component shape — in triangular units.

Work as a team to answer the following questions:

1. *a.* In triangular units, what is the total area of your panel? _____

   *b.* All the components together make up what fraction of the total area of the panel? _____

2. *a.* In triangular units, what is the area of all the triangles in your panel? _____

   *b.* Triangles make up what fraction of the total area of the panel? _____

3. *a.* In triangular units, what is the area of all the rhombuses in your panel? _____

   *b.* Rhombuses make up what fraction of the total area of the panel? _____

4. *a.* In triangular units, what is the area of all the trapezoids in your panel? _____

   *b.* Trapezoids make up what fraction of the total area of the panel? _____

5. *a.* In triangular units, what is the area of all the hexagons in your panel? _____

   *b.* Hexagons make up what fraction of the total area of the panel? _____

6. What is the sum of your answers to questions 2(*a*), 3(*a*), 4(*a*), and 5(*a*)? _____

   How does that sum compare with your answer to question 1(*a*)? _____

Navigating through Problem Solving and Reasoning in Grade 6

# Design a Spaceship Panel (continued)

Name_____

7. What is the sum of your answers to questions 2(*b*), 3(*b*), 4(*b*), and 5(*b*)?

   How does that sum compare with your answer to question 1(*b*)?

   The sum is equivalent to what whole number? _____

   Explain how you know that the fraction and the whole number are equivalent.

8. Suppose that NASA reports that the cost for building the panels is $450 per triangular unit. As a team, discuss which method of calculating the cost would be best. Use that method to determine the cost of your panel.

# Design a Cargo Bay Panel

Name_____

Suppose that you are designing the top panel for a cargo bay for NASA's new space vehicle and that your panel must consist of one hexagon, one trapezoid, one rhombus, and one triangle. Create your design with pattern blocks. Use the extra triangles in your set to measure the area of your panel — and the areas of its components — in triangular units. Then answer the following questions:

1. In triangular units, what is the total area of your cargo bay panel? _____

2. In triangular units, what is the area of the hexagon? _____

3. In triangular units, what is the area of the trapezoid? _____

4. In triangular units, what is the area of the rhombus? _____

5. In triangular units, what is the area of the triangle? _____

6. What fraction of the area of your panel is the hexagon? _____

7. What fraction of the area of your panel is the trapezoid? _____

8. What fraction of the area of your panel is the rhombus? _____

9. What fraction of the area of your panel is the triangle? _____

10. Add the fractions in your answers to questions 6, 7, 8, and 9. _____

    Your answer is equivalent to what whole number? _____

    Explain why the fraction and the whole number are equivalent. _____

11. Give at least three examples of other fractions that are equivalent to the same whole number.

Navigating through Problem Solving and Reasoning in Grade 6

# Block Buildings, Set 1 – A Constant Footprint

Names _____

_____

1. Stack centimeter cubes to create five block buildings. Each building should be one unit taller than the previous one. The drawing at the right shows the first two buildings.

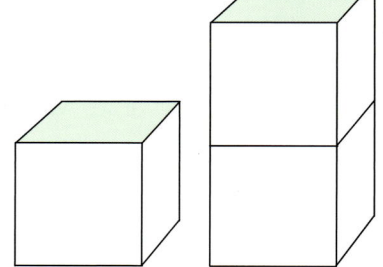

2. Find the perimeter, surface area, and volume of each building that you made in step 1, and then complete the table below. Leave the column under "$n$" blank for now.

| | Block Buildings, Set 1 | | | | | |
|---|---|---|---|---|---|---|
| | Number of the Block Building | | | | | |
| | 1 | 2 | 3 | 4 | 5 | $n$ |
| Perimeter (linear units) | | | | | | |
| Surface area (square units) | | | | | | |
| Volume (cubic units) | | | | | | |

3. Discuss the relationship between the numbers of the buildings in set 1 and the measurements of their perimeters, surface areas, and volumes. Describe each relationship in words:

   a. The relationship between a building's number and its perimeter:

   b. The relationship between a building's number and its surface area:

   c. The relationship between a building's number and its volume:

# Block Buildings, Set 1 — A Constant Footprint (continued)

Names _____

_____

Suppose that *n* stands for the number of any building. Can you use *n* in a symbolic expression, or a formula or general rule, for the perimeter, surface area, or volume of building *n*? If you can, enter your work in the last column under "*n*" in table 1.

4. Predict what a graph of each group of measurements (perimeters, surface areas, and volumes), plotted against the building numbers, would look like:

    a. A graph of the perimeters:

    b. A graph of the surface areas:

    c. A graph of the volumes:

5. On grid paper, make each of the graphs that you described in step 4.

6. A composite picture puts different pictures, or pieces of pictures, together in one picture. On grid paper, make a composite picture of the measurements of the buildings in set 1 by showing all three measurements in different colors on one graph. To do this, let your *y*-axis — the vertical axis — show "Number of Units in a Measurement" — regardless of whether they are linear units (in the perimeters), square units (in the surface areas) or cubic units (in the volumes). Let your *x*-axis — the horizontal axis — show "Building Number."

# Block Buildings, Set 2 – A Constant Height

Names _____

_____

1. Stack centimeter cubes to make a new set of five buildings. This time, let the number of square units in the bases of the buildings be equal to the squares of consecutive numbers (1 × 1, 2 × 2, 3 × 3, etc.). Make the height of each structure exactly three units. The first two buildings are shown at the right.

2. Find the perimeter, surface area, and volume of each building that you made in step 1, and then complete the table below. Leave the column under "$n$" blank for now.

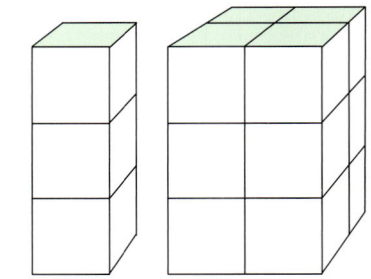

### Block Buildings, Set 2

|  | Number of the Block Building ||||||
|---|---|---|---|---|---|---|
|  | 1 | 2 | 3 | 4 | 5 | $n$ |
| Perimeter (linear units) |  |  |  |  |  |  |
| Surface area (square units) |  |  |  |  |  |  |
| Volume (cubic units) |  |  |  |  |  |  |

3. Discuss the relationship between the numbers of the buildings in set 2 and the measurements of their perimeters, surface areas, and volumes. Describe each relationship in words:

   a. The relationship between a building's number and its perimeter:

   b. The relationship between a building's number and its surface area:

   c. The relationship between a building's number and its volume:

# Block Buildings, Set 2 – A Constant Height (continued)

Names _____

_____

Suppose that *n* stands for the number of any building. Can you use *n* in a symbolic expression, or a formula or general rule, for the perimeter, surface area, or volume of building *n*? If you can, enter your work in the last column under "*n*" in table 2.

4. Predict what a graph of each group of measurements (perimeters, surface areas, and volumes), plotted against the building numbers, would look like:

   a. A graph of the perimeters:

   b. A graph of the surface areas:

   c. A graph of the volumes:

5. On grid paper, make each of the graphs that you described in step 4.

6. A *composite* picture puts different pictures, or pieces of pictures, together in one picture. On grid paper, make a composite picture of the measurements of the buildings in set 2 by showing all three measurements in different colors on one graph. To do this, let your *y*-axis — the vertical axis — show "Number of Units in a Measurement" — regardless of whether they are linear units (in the perimeters), square units (in the surface areas) or cubic units (in the volumes). Let your *x*-axis — the horizontal axis — show "Building Number."

Navigating through Problem Solving and Reasoning in Grade 6

# Block Buildings, Set 3 – Constantly Cubes

Names _____

_____

1. Stack centimeter cubes to create a set of five buildings that are successively larger cubes (1 × 1 × 1, 2 × 2 × 2, etc.). The first two buildings are shown at the right.

2. Find the perimeter, surface area, and volume of each building that you made in step 1, and then complete the table below. Leave the column under "$n$" blank for now.

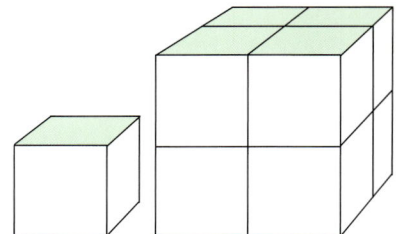

| | Block Buildings, Set 3 ||||||
|---|---|---|---|---|---|---|
| | Number of the Block Building ||||||
| | 1 | 2 | 3 | 4 | 5 | $n$ |
| Perimeter (linear units) | | | | | | |
| Surface area (square units) | | | | | | |
| Volume (cubic units) | | | | | | |

3. Discuss the relationship between the numbers of the buildings in set 3 and the measurements of their perimeters, surface areas, and volumes. Describe each relationship in words:

   a. The relationship between a building's number and its perimeter:

   b. The relationship between a building's number and its surface area:

   c. The relationship between a building's number and its volume:

Navigating through Problem Solving and Reasoning in Grade 6

# Block Buildings, Set 3 – Constantly Cubes (continued)

Names _____

_____

Suppose that *n* stands for the number of any building. Can you use *n* in a symbolic expression, or a formula or general rule, for the perimeter, surface area, or volume of building *n*? If you can, enter your work in the last column under "*n*" in table 3.

4. Predict what a graph of each group of measurements (perimeters, surface areas, and volumes), plotted against the building numbers, would look like:

   a. A graph of the perimeters:

   b. A graph of the surface areas:

   c. A graph of the volumes:

5. On grid paper, make each of the graphs that you described in step 4.

6. A composite picture puts different pictures, or pieces of pictures, together in one picture. On grid paper, make a composite picture of the measurements of the buildings in set 3 by showing all three measurements in different colors on one graph. To do this, let your *y*-axis – the vertical axis – show "Number of Units in a Measurement" – regardless of whether they are linear units (in the perimeters), square units (in the surface areas) or cubic units (in the volumes). Let your *x*-axis – the horizontal axis – show "Building Number."

# Measuring Shapes

Name_____

## Area of a Rectangle

The area of a rectangle is the number of unit squares that fill the rectangle with no gaps or overlaps.

1. Explain why the area of the rectangle below is 20 square units.

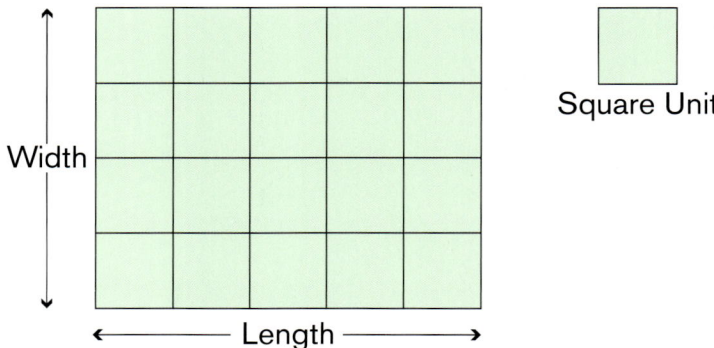

2. How can you use the dimensions of the rectangle in step 1 to find its area?

3. In general, how can you find the area of a rectangle when you know its length and width?

## Base, Altitude, and Height in a Triangle

Any side of a triangle can be its *base*. An *altitude* of a triangle is a line segment that is perpendicular to the base and joins a point on it, or on an extension of it, to the opposite vertex. The illustration below on the right shows an altitude that joins a point on an extension to the base to the opposite vertex. Note that some altitudes are inside the triangle, and others, like the one in the illustration on the right, are outside. The *height* of a triangle is the length of one of its altitudes.

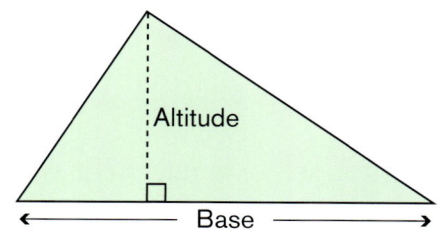 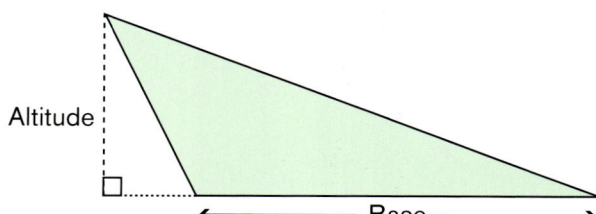

4. How many altitudes does a triangle have?

Navigating through Problem Solving and Reasoning in Grade 6

# Measuring Shapes (continued)

Name_____

## Base and Altitude in a Parallelogram

Any side of a parallelogram can be its *base*. An *altitude* of a parallelogram is a line segment that is perpendicular to the base and joins a point on it, or on an extension of it, to a point on the opposite side, or an extension of it. The illustration below shows altitudes of the parallelogram.

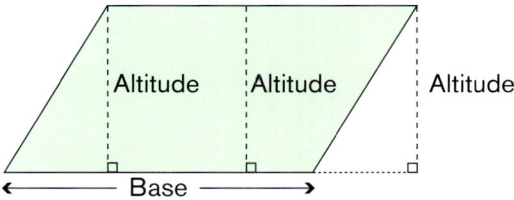

5. How many altitudes does a parallelogram have?

## Base and Altitude in a Trapezoid

A trapezoid has two parallel sides. Either of these sides can be its *base*. An *altitude* of a trapezoid is a line segment that is perpendicular to the base and joins a point on it, or an extension of it, to the opposite side, or an extension of it. The illustration below shows altitudes of the trapezoid.

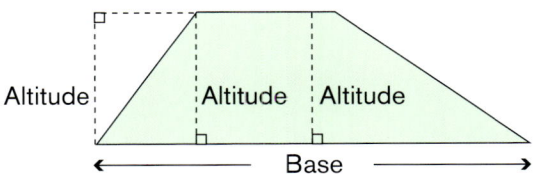

6. How many altitudes does a trapezoid have?

# Make a Rectangle from That Parallelogram

Name_____

1. *a.* On each parallelogram below, draw a line segment that divides the parallelogram into two pieces that you could rearrange to form a rectangle. To simplify the problems, be sure that all the end points of each of your line segments are on grid dots. Mark the drawings to show how you would form a rectangle from the two pieces of each parallelogram.

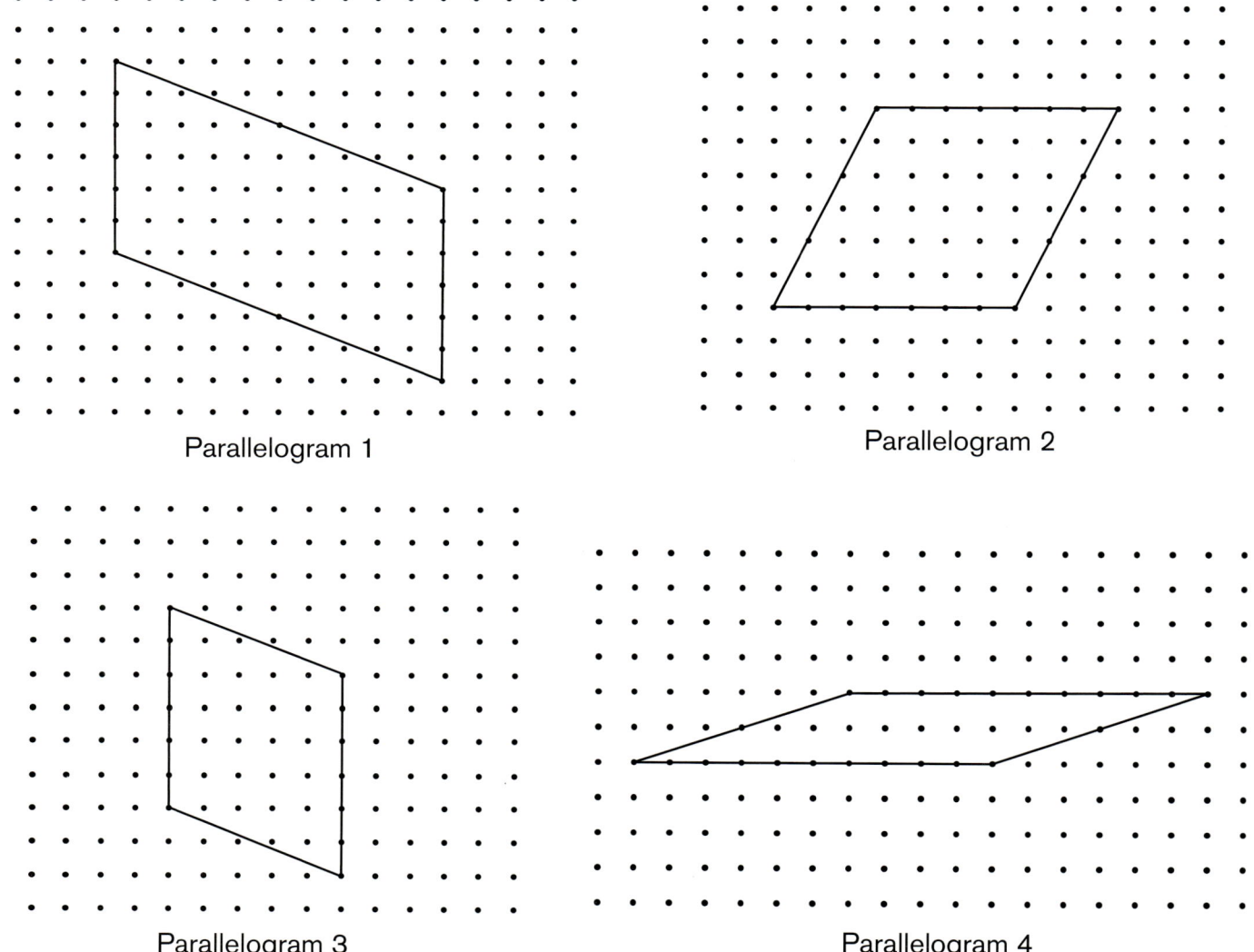

Parallelogram 1

Parallelogram 2

Parallelogram 3

Parallelogram 4

*b.* Check your ideas by actually cutting out the pieces and rearranging them or by using the 2-D Shape Decomposition Tool on a computer.

Navigating through Problem Solving and Reasoning in Grade 6

# Make a Rectangle from That Parallelogram (continued)

Name_____

2. a. Draw a line segment that divides the parallelogram below into two pieces that you could rearrange to form a rectangle. Mark on the drawing to show how you would form the rectangle from the two pieces of the parallelogram.

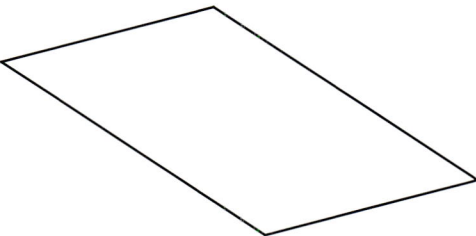

b. Check your ideas by cutting out the pieces and reassembling them or by using the 2-D Shape Decomposition Tool on your computer.

3. The formula for the area of a parallelogram is

$$Area = base \times height.$$

Use your experimentation in steps 1 and 2 to help you explain this area formula.

# Compare That Triangle with That Rectangle

Name_____

For any triangle, you can construct a rectangle that shares a base and an altitude with the triangle, as shown below.

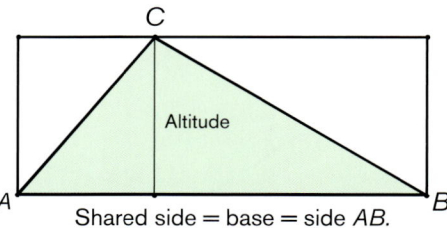

1. *a.* For each triangle below, draw a rectangle that shares a side with the triangle and has the triangle's remaining vertex as a point on the rectangle's opposite side. To simplify the problems, be sure that all the sides of your rectangles are horizontal or vertical line segments, with end points on grid dots.

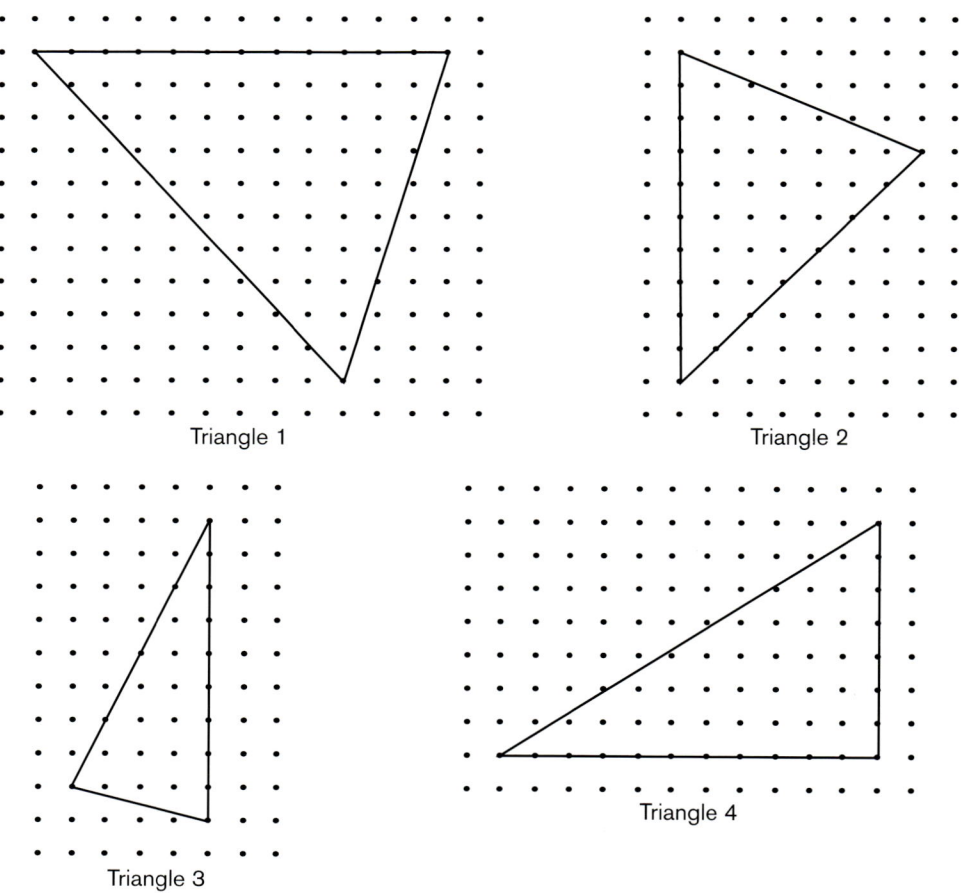

*b.* For each rectangle that you have drawn, consider how the area of the triangle compares with the area of the rectangle. Share your ideas with your partner.

# Compare That Triangle with That Rectangle (continued)

Name_____

c. Show that your ideas are correct by actually cutting out the figures and manipulating them or by using the 2-D Shape Decomposition Tool on a computer.

2. a. Draw a rectangle that shares a side with the triangle below and contains the triangle's remaining vertex as a point on its opposite side.

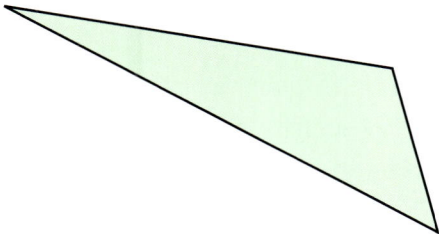

b. Describe how the area of the triangle compares with that of the rectangle.

3. The formula for the area of a triangle is

$$Area = \frac{1}{2} \; base \times height.$$

Use your experimentation in steps 1 and 2 to help you explain this area formula.

Navigating through Problem Solving and Reasoning in Grade 6

# Compare That Trapezoid with That Parallelogram

Name_____

The illustration below shows a trapezoid and marks the midpoint of one of its nonparallel sides.

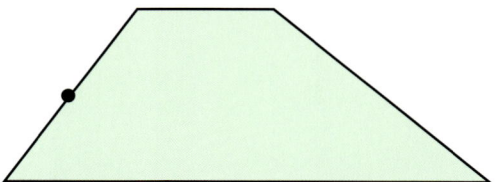

Suppose that you made an exact copy of the trapezoid and stacked it on top of your original trapezoid. Then imagine that you put a pin through both the original and your copy precisely at the marked midpoint and rotated the copy one-half turn (180 degrees). The original trapezoid and its copy — or *rotation image* — would then form the parallelogram shown below.

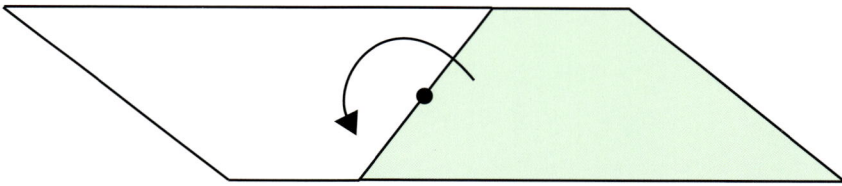

1. *a.* For each of the two trapezoids below, draw a parallelogram that you could form in the manner described above. (The midpoint is marked in the first case.)

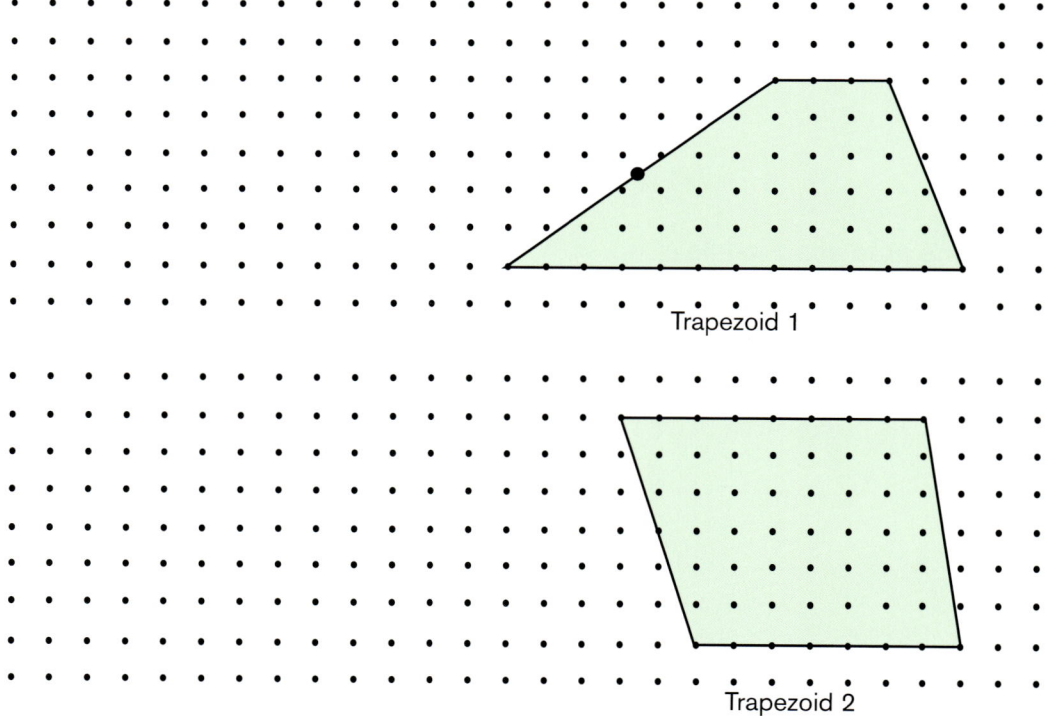

Trapezoid 1

Trapezoid 2

84  Navigating through Problem Solving and Reasoning in Grade 6

# Compare That Trapezoid with That Parallelogram (continued)

Name_____

b. How does the area of each trapezoid compare with the area of the parallelogram that you created?

c. Check your ideas by cutting out your parallelograms and the component trapezoids or by working with the 2-D Shape Decomposition Tool.

2. The formula for the area of a trapezoid is

$$Area = \frac{1}{2} \times (base\ 1 + base\ 2) \times height.$$

Discuss the process that you followed in step 1 to help you explain the area formula to your partner. Illustrate your explanation by using the diagram below to draw a parallelogram in the same way.

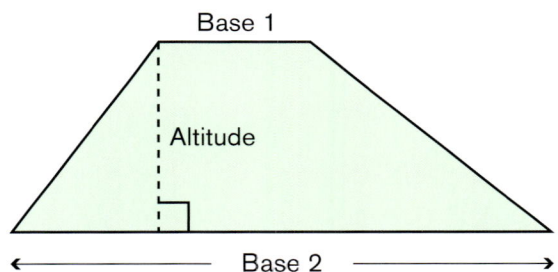

# Scale It Up, Scale It Down

Name_____

Six geometric figures appear below on dot grids. Scale each figure up or down as the activity sheet "Perimeters and Areas of Similar Figures" directs.

A.
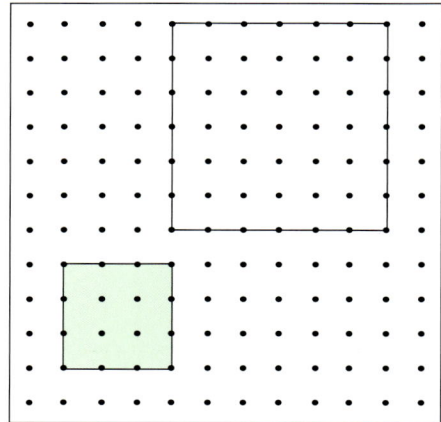

B.
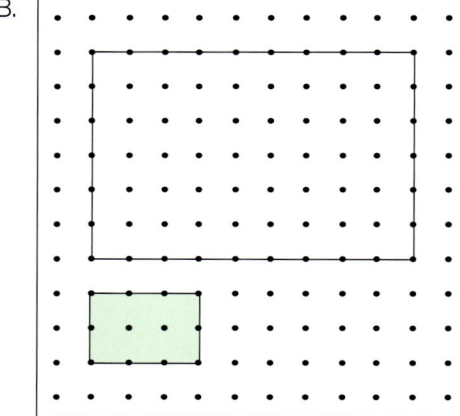

C.
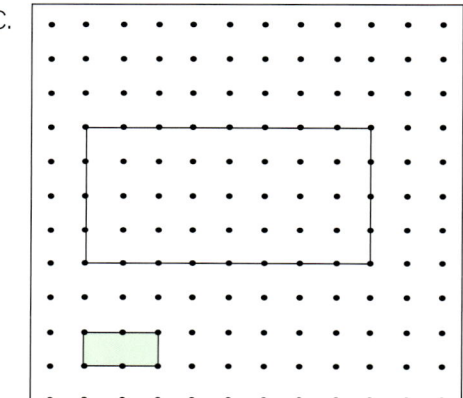

D.
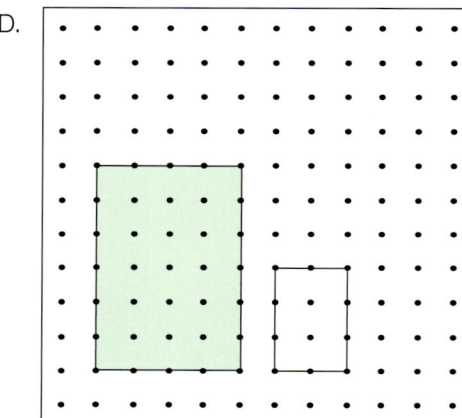

E.
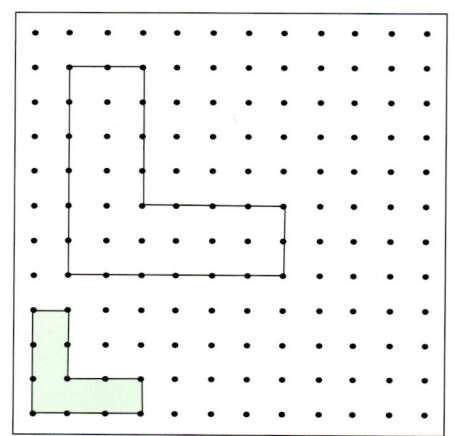

F.
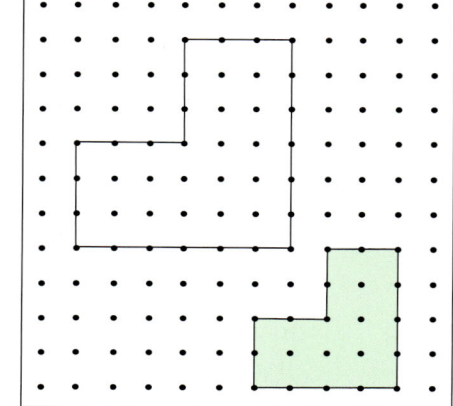

86            Navigating through Problem Solving and Reasoning in Grade 6

# Perimeters and Areas of Similar Figures

Name_____

1. The activity sheet "Scale It Up, Scale It Down" shows six geometric figures on dot grids. Column 2 in the table below shows scale factors for all the figures.

**Measurements of Preimages and Images**

| Figure | Scale Factor | Length of Longest Side in Preimage (linear units) | Length of Corresponding Side in Image (linear units) | Perimeter of Preimage (linear units) | Perimeter of Image (linear units) | Area of Preimage (square units) | Area of Image (square units) |
|---|---|---|---|---|---|---|---|
| A | 2 | | | | | | |
| B | 3 | | | | | | |
| C | 4 | | | | | | |
| D | $\frac{1}{2}$ | | | | | | |
| E | 2 | | | | | | |
| F | $\frac{3}{2}$ | | | | | | |

a. For each figure (called a *preimage*), locate the appropriate scale factor, and use it to draw a similar figure (called an *image*) on the same grid as the preimage on "Scale It Up, Scale It Down."

b. Complete the table:
- Identify the longest side in each preimage, and determine its length. Find the corresponding side in each image, and determine its length. Record your results.
- Determine the perimeter of each preimage. Then determine the perimeter of each image. Record your results.
- Determine the area of each preimage. Then determine the area of each image. Record your results.

# Perimeters and Areas of Similar Figures (continued)

Name_____

2. *a.* For each figure, find the ratio of the length of the longest side of the image to the length of the longest side of the preimage.

A_____  D_____

B_____  E_____

C_____  F_____

*b.* What patterns do you observe in the ratios? _____

_____

_____

3. *a.* For each figure, find the ratio of the perimeter of the image to the perimeter of the preimage.

A_____  D_____

B_____  E_____

C_____  F_____

*b.* What patterns do you observe in the ratios? _____

_____

_____

4. *a.* For each figure, find the ratio of the area of the image to the area of the preimage.

A_____  D_____

B_____  E_____

C_____  F_____

*b.* What patterns do you observe in the ratios? _____

_____

_____

# Perimeters and Areas of Similar Figures (continued)

Name_____

5. Consider the patterns that you observed in steps 2–4.

   a. What conclusions can you draw about corresponding sides, perimeters, and areas of similar figures? (*Hint*: Use the scale factor in your explanation.)

   b. Suppose that a figure has a perimeter of 13 units and an area of 16 square units and you are going to enlarge it on a copy machine by using a scale factor of 250%. What will the perimeter and area of your enlarged figure be?

   P = _____

   A = _____

   How did you get your answers?

6. (Optional) A pizza restaurant sells two different sizes of pizza — a small one that is 6 inches in diameter and a large one that is 12 inches in diameter. The small pizza costs $5. If the restaurant prices its pizzas proportionally by their areas, what should the price of the large pizza be?

# Surface Areas and Volumes of Similar Figures

Name_____

1. *a.* Use centimeter cubes to build the geometric figure A, whose dimensions (*length × width × height*, in centimeters) appear in column 2 in the table. The figure is a three-dimensional box—a *rectangular prism*. Use the scale factor given in column 3 to build a second rectangular prism that is the *image* of figure A (the *preimage*). Find the surface areas and volumes of the preimage and image and enter them to complete the row for figure A.

**Measurements of Preimages and Images**

| Figure (Preimage) | Dimensions of Preimage (centimeters) | Scale Factor | Surface Area of Preimage (square centimeters) | Surface Area of Image (square centimeters) | Volume of Preimage (cubic centimeters) | Volume of Image (cubic centimeters) |
|---|---|---|---|---|---|---|
| A | 1 × 2 × 3 | 2 | | | | |
| B | 1 × 2 × 1 | 3 | | | | |
| C | 1 × 1 × 1 | 4 | | | | |
| D | 2 × 2 × 4 | $\frac{1}{2}$ | | | | |
| E | 4 × 2 × 4 | $\frac{3}{2}$ | | | | |

*b.* Repeat the process that you followed in (*a*), this time building figure B and its image, as specified in the table. Then complete the row for figure B by finding and recording the surface areas and volumes of your new preimage and image.

*c.* Repeat the process, building figures C, D, and E in turn and completing the respective rows in the table. You may need to dismantle figures and images that you built earlier to have enough cubes to build new ones.

# Surface Areas and Volumes of Similar Figures (continued)

Name_____

2. *a.* For each figure, find the ratio of the surface area of the image to the surface area of the preimage.

   A_____          D_____

   B_____          E_____

   C_____          F_____

   *b.* What patterns do you observe?

3. *a.* For each figure, find the ratio of the volume of the image to the volume of the preimage.

   A_____          D_____

   B_____          E_____

   C_____          F_____

   *b.* What patterns do you observe?

4. Consider the patterns that you observed in steps 2 and 3. What conclusions can you draw about the surface areas and volumes of similar figures? (*Hint:* Use the scale factor in your explanation.)

5. Suppose that a building has a volume of 100,000 cubic feet and you have been assigned to build a scale model of the building by using a scale factor of $\frac{1}{100}$. What will the volume of your scale model be?

   V = _____

   How did you arrive at your answer?

# Scale Models

Name_____

People who make models of objects use a *scale factor* to determine the size of each part that they make for the model. The scale factor is a ratio that gives the mathematical relationship between lengths in the model and corresponding lengths in its life-sized counterpart. For instance, an O gauge model train has a scale factor of 1:48, or $\frac{1}{48}$, which means that each inch of the model corresponds to 48 inches on the original train. Makers of models use scale factors to ensure that a replica is like the original object in all of its proportions.

Suppose that you buy a model train engine and you see on the package that 1 inch in the model equals 10 feet in the actual engine. What is the scale factor? Remember that a scale factor is a ratio and has no units. You can convert one of these measurements to express both in the same units. Ten feet equals 120 inches, so you can express the relationship this way:

$$\frac{1 \text{ inch}}{10 \text{ feet}} = \frac{1 \text{ inch}}{120 \text{ inches}} = \frac{1}{120}.$$

1. In an HO model train set, 1 inch is 7.25 feet. What is the scale factor?

   Explain your thinking.

2. The scale on a county map reads, "1 inch equals 25 miles." What is the scale factor?

   Explain your thinking.

Navigating through Problem Solving and Reasoning in Grade 6

# Scale Models (continued)

Name _____

3. In Jonathan Swift's great classic, *Gulliver's Travels*, the shipwrecked hero, Gulliver, washes up in Lilliput, an island nation of people who are perfectly proportioned but not quite 6 inches high. Suppose that a Lilliputian is exactly 6 inches tall and Gulliver is exactly 6 feet.

   a. What is the scale factor between the Lilliputian and Gulliver?

   Explain your thinking.

   b. Imagine a mattress on which Gulliver could sleep comfortably in his own house after a sea voyage. Imagine a scaled-down mattress on which the Lilliputian could sleep with equal room. What are the dimensions of the two mattress tops, and how do their areas compare?

   Explain your thinking.

   c. Imagine Gulliver at home in his living room — which he might call his "parlor" or "sitting room." What might the room's dimensions be? What would the dimensions of a scaled-down room for the Lilliputian be? How would the volume of Gulliver's room compare to the volume of the Lilliputian's room?

   Explain your thinking.

Navigating through Problem Solving and Reasoning in Grade 6

# Scale Models (continued)

Name_____

4. On grid paper, draw a person or object or create a design. Choose a scale factor that you can use to make an image of your drawing on the same sheet of grid paper. Estimate the areas of your drawing and its image. Provide the following information about your similar figures.

Scale factor: _____

Approximate area of preimage: _____

Approximate area of image: _____

Comparison of areas: _____

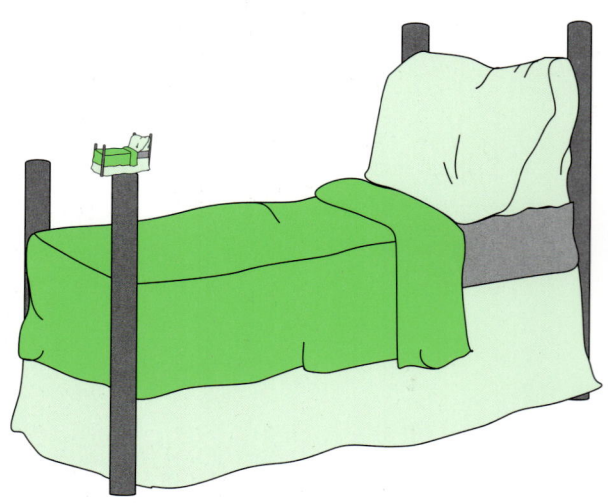

# Fun on the Field

Each year, Washington Elementary and Junior High School dedicates a month to personal fitness. Teachers, students, parents, and administrators all discuss the benefits of a healthy lifestyle. During the month, the school invites guest lecturers, including famous athletes and health professionals, to give talks and demonstrate their skills and knowledge. Students and alumni participate in a host of physical events. New additions to the festivities this year include a parents vs. students baseball game, a teachers vs. students basketball game, and a community walkathon. The school will conclude its monthlong celebration of personal fitness with Fitness Field Day.

Fitness Field Day is a one-day festival during which students compete in many outdoor sports events. Fifth grader David Marcett said, "I love FF Day, and I wouldn't miss it for the world! The whole school community gets together to watch us in the contests." When asked about his favorite events, David enthusiastically declared his choice: "Track and field!" He added, "Out of all the competitions, I know everyone likes the track and field contests the best. They're the ones that really test our personal fitness."

David is not alone in his preference. The organizers of the Fitness Field Day expect the track and field contests to be the most popular. These contests will be divided into three major groups: running, jumping, and throwing. The running contests will consist of sprints and relay races. The throwing competitions will include the shot put, the discus throw, and the javelin throw. Contests in the long jump and the high jump will test the students' jumping skills.

Hurdle racing involves both running and jumping and cannot be classified simply as one or the other. Thus, it will occupy a category by itself in the festival.

The Fitness Field Day organizers are working very hard to ensure that all the teams will be approximately equal in ability so that all the competitions will be fair and everyone will have fun.

---

The development of this activity was supported by the School Mathematics and Science Center (SMSC), Purdue University, West Lafayette, Indiana, under the direction of Richard Lesh.

# Fielding the Facts

Name_____

1. What is Fitness Field Day?

2. What would be an advantage of having Fitness Field Day at the school?

3. Which sporting events do the organizers of Fitness Field Day expect to be the most popular?

4. Why do you think the Fitness Field Day organizers want to ensure that all the teams are approximately equal in ability?

5. Look at the table below. Which student has the best time for the 800 meter race?

**Sixth Graders' Fitness Scores**

| Student | 800-Meter Run | High Jump |
| --- | --- | --- |
| Betsy | 3 min 38 sec | 5'3" |
| Dick | 2 min 55 sec | 4'4" |
| Jason | 2 min 55 sec | 3'9" |
| Judi | 3 min 22 sec | 3'6" |
| Manuel | 3 min 11 sec | 4'2" |
| Margret | 2 min 51 sec | 5'7" |
| Michelle | 2 min 45 sec | 4'5" |
| Rob | 3 min 12 sec | 4'10" |
| Scott | 3 min 30 sec | 4'11" |
| Susan | 3 min 0 sec | 5'3" |

6. In the table in step 5, which student's performance was weakest in the high jump event? How high did this student jump?

---

The development of this activity was supported by the School Mathematics and Science Center (SMSC), Purdue University, West Lafayette, Indiana, under the direction of Richard Lesh.

# Fitness Fest Investigation

Name_____

*The situation:* Washington Elementary and Junior High School will soon hold its annual Fitness Field Day. However, the organizers of the festival still must assign the sixth- and seventh-grade athletes to teams for the track and field events. The organizers want to be sure that all the teams entering these events are roughly equal in ability. They have collected data on the performances of each track and field athlete in the sixth and seventh grades. Their data on the sixth-grade athletes appear in the table below.

## Sixth Graders' Fitness Scores

| Student | 100-Meter Run | 800-Meter Run | High Jump | Fitness Test* |
|---|---|---|---|---|
| Betsy | 17.3 sec | 3 min 38 sec | 5'3" | Pass |
| Caroline | 16.0 sec | 3 min 1 sec | 3'5" | Fail |
| Daniel | 19.89 sec | 2 min 42 sec | 5'5" | Pass |
| Dick | 18.52 sec | 2 min 55 sec | 4'4" | Pass |
| Jason | 16.48 sec | 2 min 55 sec | 3'9" | Pass |
| Judi | 17.2 sec | 3 min 22 sec | 3'6" | Fail |
| Linda | 20.2 sec | 4 min 0 sec | 5'0" | Pass |
| Mack | 18.25 sec | 3 min 16 sec | 5'6" | Pass |
| Manuel | 17.1 sec | 3 min 11 sec | 4'2" | Fail |
| Margret | 20.32 sec | 2 min 51 sec | 5'7" | Pass |
| Michelle | 16.44 sec | 2 min 45 sec | 4'5" | Fail |
| Rob | 19.2 sec | 3 min 12 sec | 4'10" | Fail |
| Sandra | 17.34 sec | 3 min 50 sec | 5'1" | Fail |
| Scott | 17.0 sec | 3 min 30 sec | 4'11" | Pass |
| Susan | 18.3 sec | 3 min 0 sec | 5'3" | Pass |

*All students received a mark of "pass" or "fail." The test consisted of 30 push-ups, 50 jumping jacks, and 20 sit-ups.

The development of this activity was supported by the School Mathematics and Science Center (SMSC), Purdue University, West Lafayette, Indiana, under the direction of Richard Lesh.

# Fitness Fest Investigation (continued)

Name_____

*The problem*: Help the organizers with their work. Use their data to develop a method for assigning the sixth-grade participants to three teams that you would expect to be roughly equal in ability. Work on this problem with the other members of your group.

*What's next?* When all the groups have developed their methods, each one will present its teams and give a step-by-step explanation of its procedure for determining them. As each group makes its presentation, the members of all the other groups will play the roles of organizers of Fitness Field Day. They will ask questions, and then they will evaluate the method by testing it on new data. Using data on the seventh-grade participants in Fitness Field Day, they will apply the method to assign these participants to teams.

*The impact:* After all the groups have made their presentations, each one will revise and improve its method. The organizers of Fitness Field Day hope to identify an effective method that they can recommend to all the schools in the district for use in all the annual field day competitions. When your group has finalized its method, all the team members should work together to write a letter to the coordinator of the organizing committee — your teacher — explaining the group's procedure and highlighting its advantages.

# Seventh-Grade Performance Data

Name_____

## Seventh Graders' Fitness Scores

| Student | 100-Meter Run | 800-Meter Run | High Jump | Fitness Test* |
|---|---|---|---|---|
| Matt | 16.3 sec | 2 min 55 sec | 3'8" | Pass |
| Eleanor | 18.35 sec | 3 min 0 sec | 5'2" | Pass |
| Damian | 20.1 sec | 2 min 50 sec | 5'8" | Pass |
| Tad | 17.4 sec | 3 min 40 sec | 5'3" | Pass |
| Alexa | 16.1 sec | 3 min 50 sec | 5'5" | Pass |
| Mallory | 17.38 sec | 2 min 45 sec | 5'1" | Fail |
| George | 18.81 sec | 2 min 56 sec | 4'2" | Pass |
| Daria | 17.2 sec | 3 min 25 sec | 3'5" | Fail |
| Lucas | 20.4 sec | 4 min 0 sec | 5'0" | Pass |
| Edward | 16.39 sec | 2 min 46 sec | 4'7" | Fail |
| Maureen | 18.81 sec | 3 min 17 sec | 5'5" | Pass |
| Carlos | 17.0 sec | 3 min 29 sec | 4'11" | Pass |
| Becky | 17.15 sec | 3 min 10 sec | 4'4" | Fail |
| Nick | 18.2 sec | 3 min 12 sec | 4'9" | Fail |
| Gina | 19.9 sec | 3 min 1 sec | 3'6" | Fail |

*All students received a mark of "pass" or "fail." The test consisted of 30 push-ups, 50 jumping jacks, and 20 sit-ups.

---

The development of this activity was supported by the School Mathematics and Science Center (SMSC), Purdue University, West Lafayette, Indiana, under the direction of Richard Lesh.

# Solutions for the Blackline Masters

## Solutions for "Finding Triangular Area"

1–2. The area of the polygon is twenty-four triangular units.

## Solutions for "Design a Spaceship Panel"

1. *a.* Answers will vary according to each team's design.

   *b.* Answers will vary according to each team's design, but the fraction should be equivalent to 1.

2–5. Answers will vary according to each team's design.

6. The sum will vary according to each team's design. The sum should equal the answer to question 1(*a*).

7. The fraction will vary according to each team's design, but it should be equivalent to 1. The sum should be equivalent to the answer to question 1(*b*). The sum should be equivalent to the number 1. Various explanations of the equivalence are acceptable, including the principle that a number divided by itself equals 1. The students might also refer to their panels or other models or to a number line to demonstrate equivalence.

8. The costs will vary.

## Solutions for "Design a Cargo Bay Panel"

1. The area of the panel is twelve triangular units.
2. The area of the hexagon is six triangular units.
3. The area of the trapezoid is three triangular units.
4. The area of the rhombus is two triangular units.
5. The area of the triangle is one triangular unit.
6. The hexagon is 6/12, or 1/2 the area of the panel.
7. The trapezoid is 3/12, or 1/4 the area of the panel.
8. The rhombus is 2/12, or 1/6 the area of the panel.
9. The triangle is 1/12 the area of the panel.
10. The sum of the fractions is 12/12, which is equivalent to 1. Various explanations of the equivalence are acceptable, including the principle that a number divided by itself equals 1; the students might also refer to their panels or other models or to a number line to demonstrate equivalence.
11. Answers will vary, but all answers should equal 1.

Solutions for Blackline Masters

# Solutions for "Block Buildings, Set 1 – A Constant Footprint"

1. The first five block buildings in set 1 appear below.

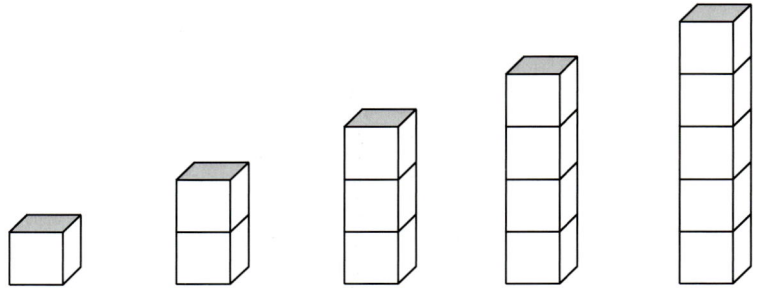

2. The completed table for the first five block buildings in set 1 is shown.

| | Block Buildings, Set 1 | | | | | |
|---|---|---|---|---|---|---|
| | Number of the Block Building | | | | | |
| | 1 | 2 | 3 | 4 | 5 | $n$ |
| Perimeter (linear units) | 12 | 16 | 20 | 24 | 28 | $4n + 8$, or $4(n + 2)$ |
| Surface area (square units) | 6 | 10 | 14 | 18 | 22 | $4n + 2$, or $2(2n + 1)$ |
| Volume (cubic units) | 1 | 2 | 3 | 4 | 5 | $n$ |

3. *a.* The perimeter increases by four linear units with each successive building.

   *b.* The surface area increases by four square units with each successive building.

   *c.* The volume increases by one cubic unit with each successive building.

4. *a–c.* The correct prediction is that the graphs of each set of measurements (perimeter, surface area, and volume) will all be straight lines.

5–6. A graph of the perimeters, surface areas, and volumes of the buildings in set 1 appears on the next page.

## Block Buildings, Set 1

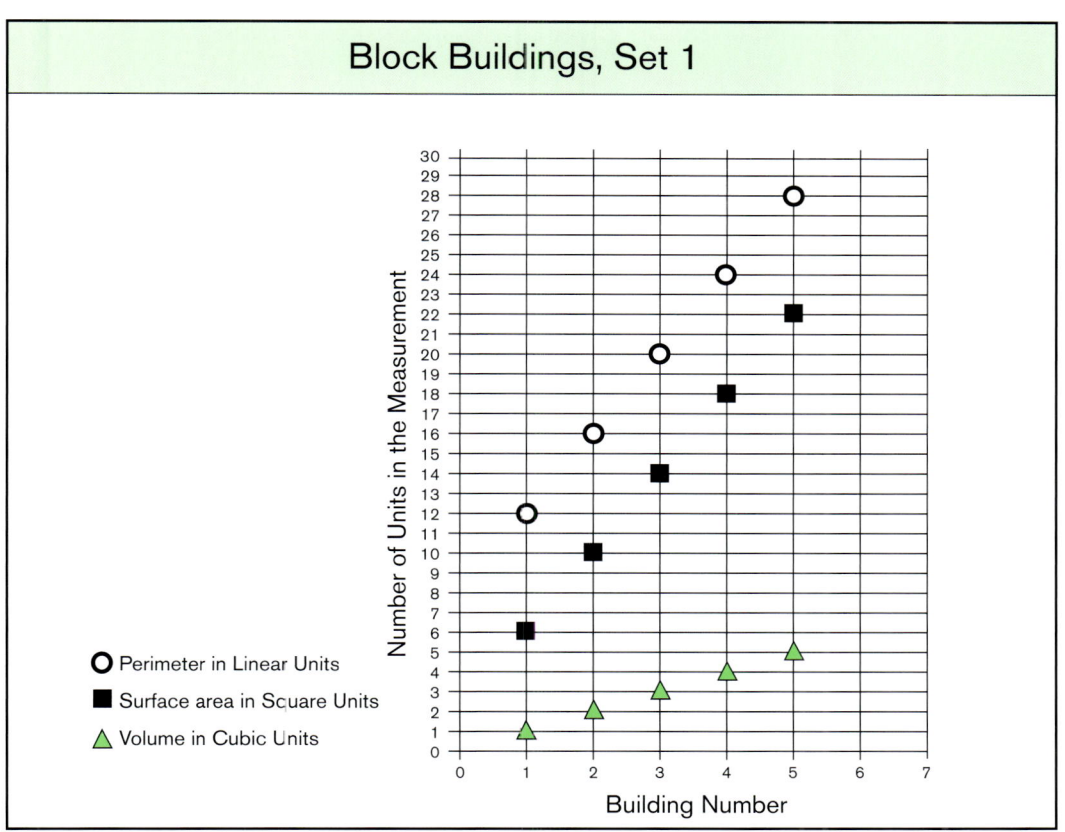

## Solutions for "Block Buildings, Set 2 – A Constant Height"

1. The first five block buildings in set 2 appear on below.

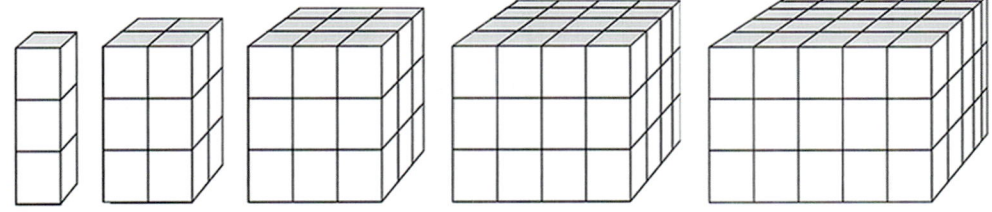

2. The completed table for the first five block buildings in set 2 is shown.

| Block Buildings, Set 2 | | | | | | |
|---|---|---|---|---|---|---|
| | Number of the Block Building | | | | | |
| | 1 | 2 | 3 | 4 | 5 | $n$ |
| Perimeter (linear units) | 20 | 28 | 36 | 44 | 52 | $8n + 12$, or $4(2n + 3)$ |
| Surface area (square units) | 14 | 32 | 54 | 80 | 110 | $2n^2 + 12n$, or $2n(n+6)$ |
| Volume (cubic units) | 3 | 12 | 27 | 48 | 75 | $3n^2$ |

Solutions for Blackline Masters

3. *a.* The perimeter increases by eight linear units with each successive building. (See below, column 2.)

   *b.* The difference between two successive values for surface area increases by four square units for successive pairs of buildings. (The second differences are constant; see below, column 3.)

   *c.* The difference between two successive values for volume increases by six cubic units for successive pairs of buildings. (The second differences are constant; see below, column 4.)

| Building | Perimeter | Surface Area | Volume |
|---|---|---|---|
| 5 | 52 | 110 | 75 |
| 4 | 44 | 80 | 48 |
| 3 | 36 | 54 | 27 |
| 2 | 28 | 32 | 12 |
| 1 | 20 | 14 | 3 |

Perimeter successive differences: 8, 8, 8, 8 (a)

Surface Area successive differences: 30, 26, 22, 18 with second differences 4, 4, 4 (b)

Volume successive differences: 27, 21, 15, 9 with second differences 6, 6, 6 (c)

4. The correct predictions are that the graph of the measurements for perimeter will be a straight line and the graphs of the measurements for surface area and volume will be curves.

5–6. A graph of the perimeters, surface areas, and volumes of the buildings in set 2 appears below.

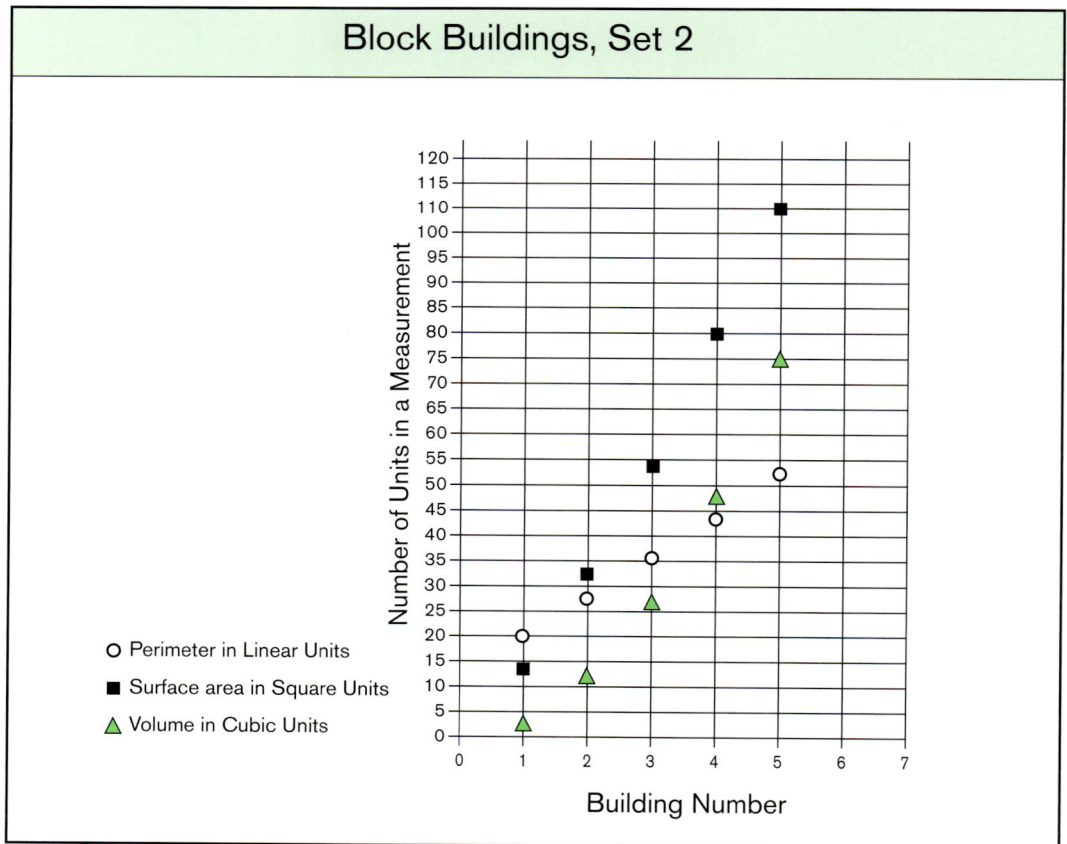

Block Buildings, Set 2

○ Perimeter in Linear Units
■ Surface area in Square Units
▲ Volume in Cubic Units

# Solutions for "Block Buildings, Set 3– Constantly Cubes"

1. The first five block buildings in set 3 appear below.

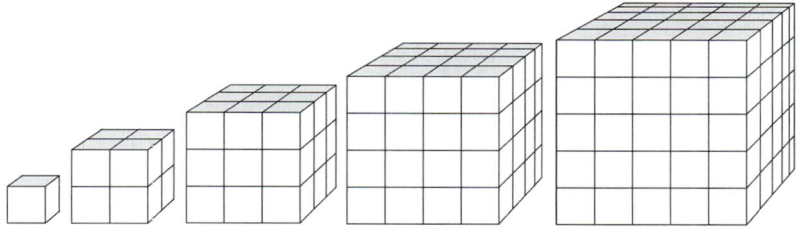

2. The completed table for the first five block buildings in set 3 is shown.

| | Block Buildings, Set 3 | | | | | |
|---|---|---|---|---|---|---|
| | Number of the Block Building | | | | | |
| | 1 | 2 | 3 | 4 | 5 | $n$ |
| Perimeter (linear units) | 12 | 24 | 36 | 48 | 60 | $12n$ |
| Surface area (square units) | 6 | 24 | 54 | 96 | 150 | $6n^2$ |
| Volume (cubic units) | 1 | 8 | 27 | 64 | 125 | $n^3$ |

3. a. The perimeter increases by twelve linear units with each successive building. (See below, column 2.)

   b. The difference between two successive values for surface area increases by twelve square units for successive pairs of buildings. (The second differences are constant; see below, column 3.)

   c. The difference between the differences between two successive values for volume increases by six cubic units for successive pairs of buildings. (The third differences are constant; see below, column 4.)

| Building | Perimeter | Surface Area | Volume |
|---|---|---|---|
| 5 | 60 | 150 | 125 |
| | 12 | 54 | 61 |
| 4 | 48 | 96 | 64 | 
| | 12 | 42 / 12 | 37 / 24 |
| 3 | 36 | 54 | 27 | 
| | 12 | 30 / 12 | 19 / 18, 6 |
| 2 | 24 | 24 | 8 |
| | 12 | 18 / 12 | 7 / 12, 6 |
| 1 | 12 | 6 | 1 |
| | (a) | (b) | (c) |

4. The correct predictions are that the graph of the measurements for perimeter will be a straight line and the graphs of the measurements for surface area and volume will be curves.

5–6. A graph of the perimeters, surface areas, and volumes of the buildings in set 3 appears below.

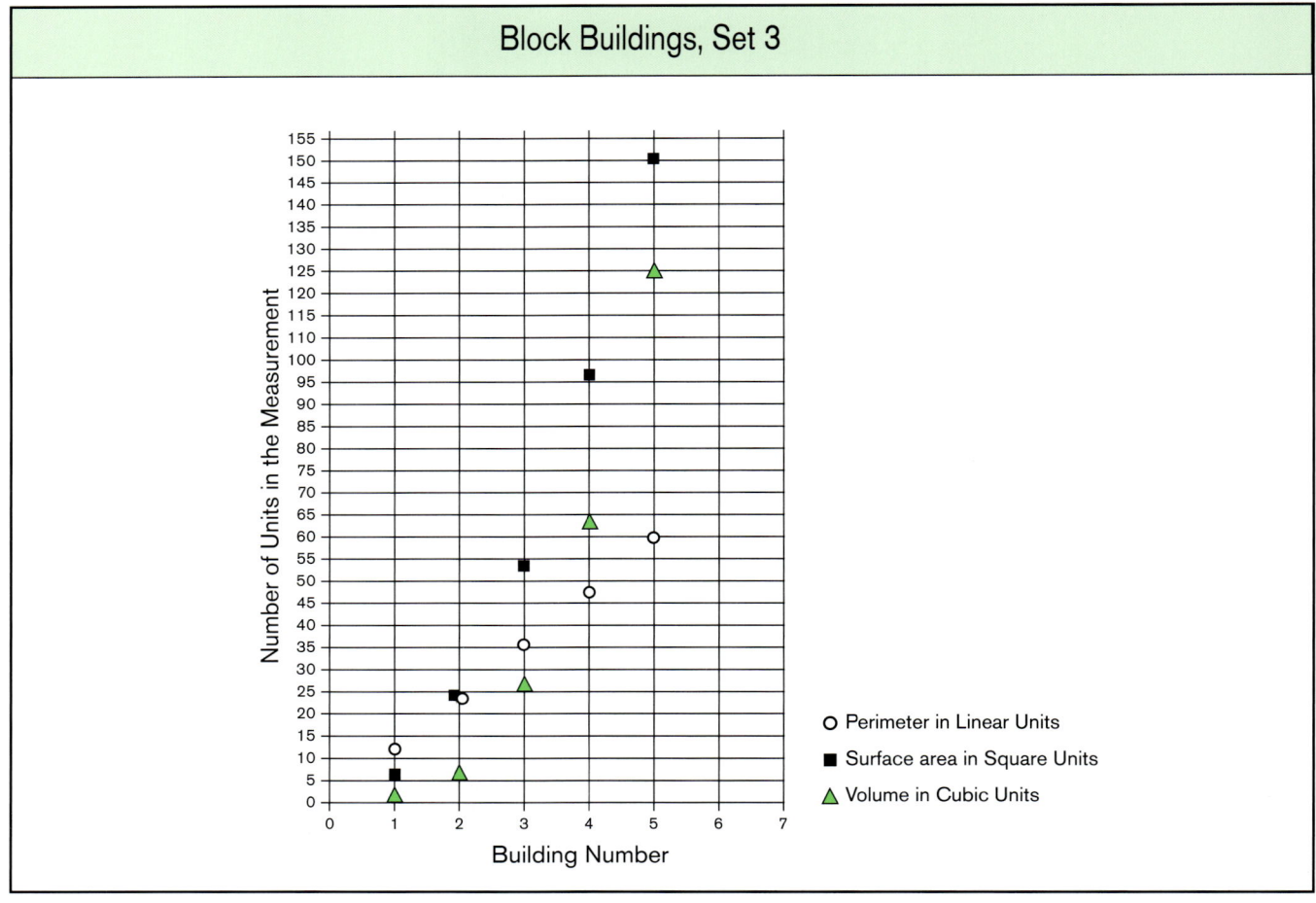

# Solutions for "Measuring Shapes"

1. The area of the rectangle is 20 square units because twenty unit squares fill the rectangle exactly, with no gaps or overlaps.

2. The rectangle has five unit squares in each row, and it has four rows; $5 \times 4 = 20$, so the area is 20 square units.

3. The area of a rectangle is the product of its length and its width.

4. A triangle has three altitudes.

5. A parallelogram has an infinite number of altitudes.

6. A trapezoid has an infinite number of altitudes.

# Solutions for "Make a Rectangle from That Parallelogram"

1. Examples of correct solutions for the parallelograms are illustrated on the next page. Other solutions are possible.

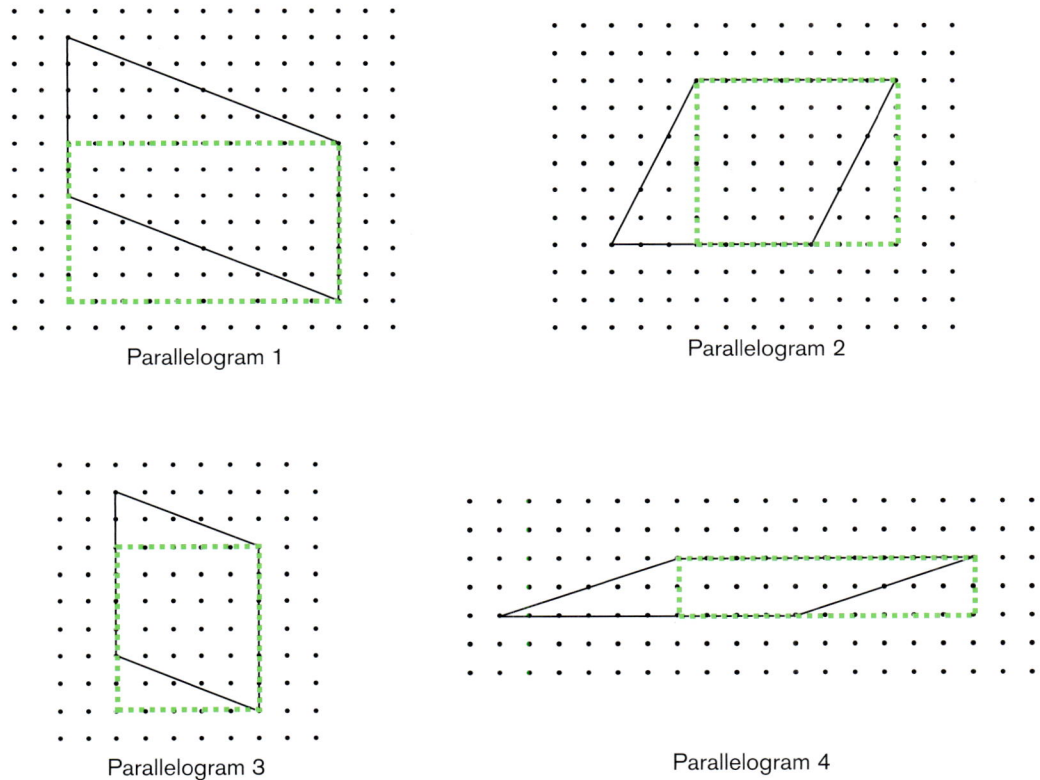

Parallelogram 1

Parallelogram 2

Parallelogram 3

Parallelogram 4

2. The illustration below shows a line segment that divides the parallelogram into two pieces that could be recomposed as a rectangle. Other solutions are possible.

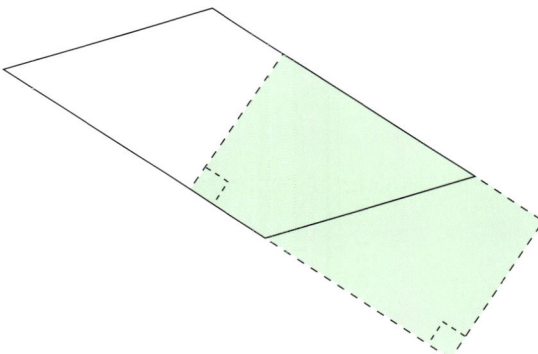

3. Students' explanations will vary but should include the idea that cutting a parallelogram along any of its interior altitudes produces two pieces can be recomposed as a rectangle. The rectangle has not only the same area as the parallelogram but also the same base and height, allowing for a simple restatement of the formula for the area of a rectangle that applies it to a parallelogram.

# Solutions for "Compare That Triangle with That Rectangle"

1. Examples of correct solutions for the triangles are illustrated on the next page.

Solutions for Blackline Masters

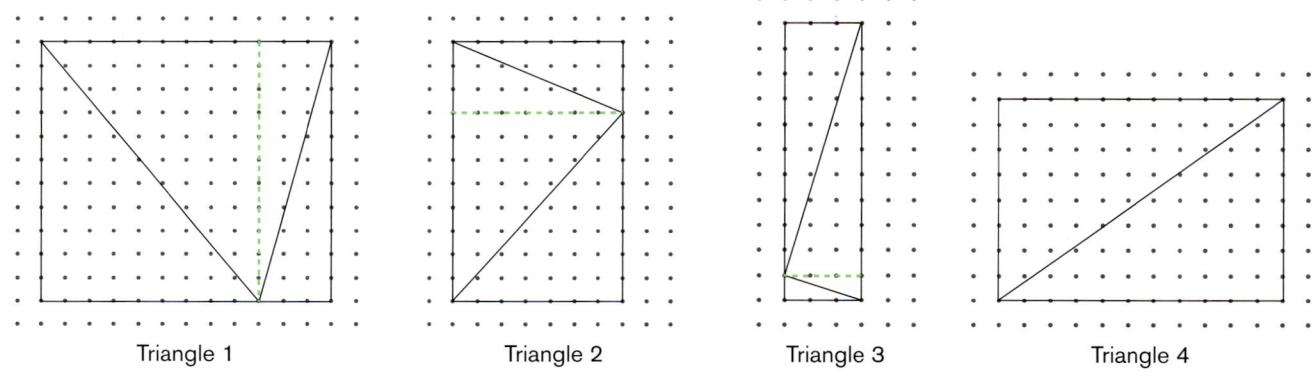

| Triangle 1 | Triangle 2 | Triangle 3 | Triangle 4 |

2. The correct solution is shown to the right.

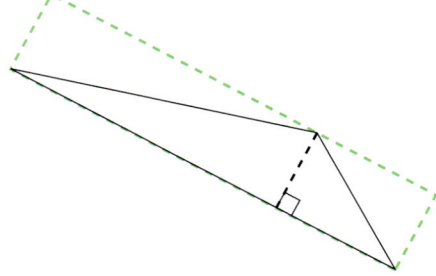

3. The students' work in steps 1 and 2 should have demonstrated to them that the area of each triangle is one-half of the area of the corresponding rectangle, and they should be able to use the formula for the area of a rectangle to derive the formula for the area of a triangle.

## Solutions for "Compare That Trapezoid with That Parallelogram"

1. Examples of correct solutions for the trapezoids are illustrated below. Another example is possible in each case.

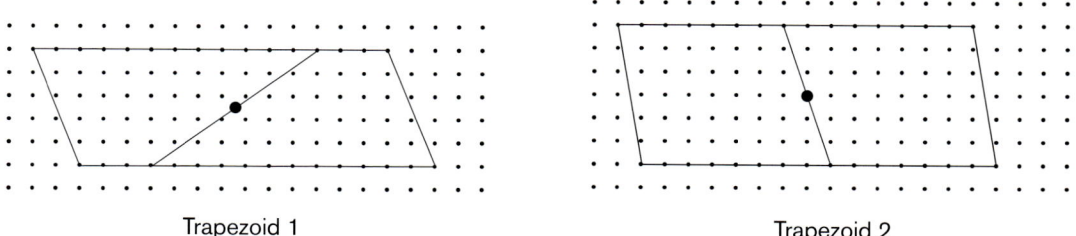

| Trapezoid 1 | Trapezoid 2 |

2. In step 1, the students discovered that they can form a parallelogram with a trapezoid and its rotation image. They can produce the parallelogram shown below.

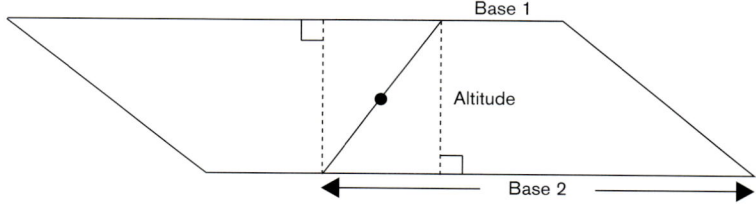

Because the rotation image has the same area as the original trapezoid, each trapezoid has one-half of the area of the parallelogram. The students can use the formula that they derived earlier for the area of a parallelogram to derive the formula for the area of a trapezoid.

# Solutions for "Scale It Up, Scale It Down"

The students use the scale factors given in the table on the activity sheet "Perimeters and Areas of Similar Figures" to produce the images shown below for the geometric figures on dot grids.

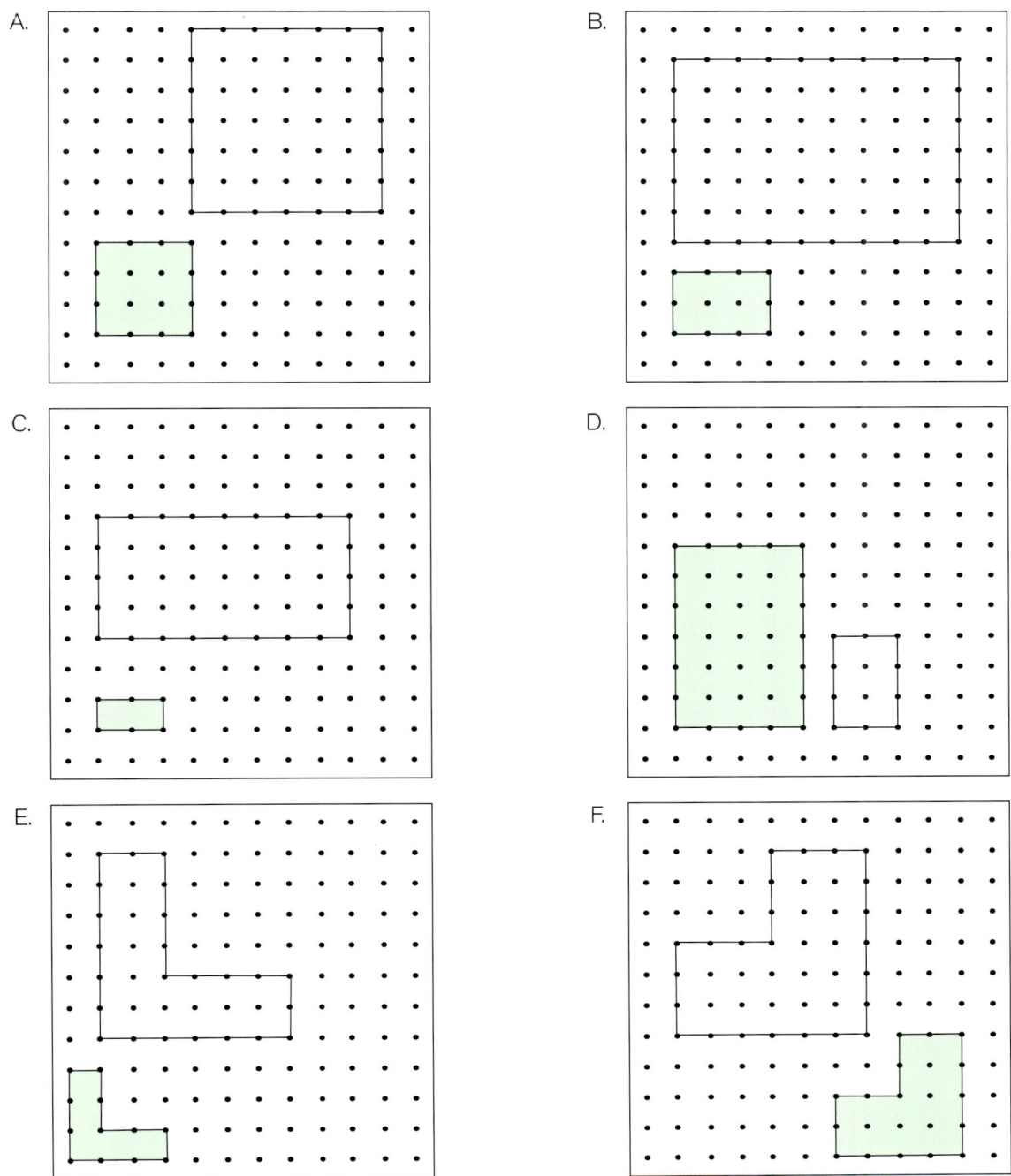

Solutions for Blackline Masters

# Solutions for "Perimeters and Areas of Similar Figures"

1. After drawing images according to the given scale factors for the preimages on dot grids on "Scale It Up, Scale It Down," the students complete the table as shown.

**Measurements of Preimages and Images**

| Figure | Scale Factor | Length of Longest Side in Preimage (linear units) | Length of Corresponding Side in Image (linear units) | Perimeter of Preimage (linear units) | Perimeter of Image (linear units) | Area of Preimage (square units) | Area of Image (square units) |
|---|---|---|---|---|---|---|---|
| A | 2 | 3 | 6 | 12 | 24 | 9 | 36 |
| B | 3 | 3 | 9 | 10 | 30 | 6 | 54 |
| C | 4 | 2 | 8 | 6 | 24 | 2 | 32 |
| D | $\frac{1}{2}$ | 6 | 3 | 20 | 10 | 24 | 6 |
| E | 2 | 3 | 6 | 12 | 24 | 5 | 20 |
| F | $\frac{3}{2}$ | 4 | 6 | 16 | 24 | 12 | 27 |

2. For each figure, A–F, the students should discover that the ratio of the lengths of the longest sides of the image and the preimage is the scale factor.

3. For each figure, A–F, the students should discover that the ratio of the corresponding perimeters of the image and the preimage is the scale factor.

4. For each figure, A–F, the students should discover that the ratio of the corresponding areas of the image and the preimage is the square of the scale factor.

5. *a.* Students should state their conclusions clearly: the ratio of the length of a side of an image to the length of the corresponding side of its preimage is the scale factor, the ratio of the perimeter of an image to the perimeter of its preimage is the scale factor, and the ratio of the area of an image to the area of its preimage is the square of the scale factor.

   *b.* The perimeter of the image will be $13 \times 2.5 = 32.5$ units. The area of the image will be $16 \times (2.5)^2 = 100$ square units.

6. The scale factor is 2. The price of the pizza depends on its area. The ratio of the areas is the square of the scale factor. So the large pizza should cost $5 \times 2^2 = \$20$.

# Solutions for "Surface Areas and Volumes of Similar Figures"

1. The completed table appears below.

**Measurements of Preimages and Images**

| Figure (Preimage) | Dimensions of Preimage (centimeters) | Scale Factor | Surface Area of Preimage (square centimeters) | Surface Area of Image (square centimeters) | Volume of Preimage (cubic centimeters) | Volume of Image (cubic centimeters) |
|---|---|---|---|---|---|---|
| A | 1 × 2 × 3 | 2 | 22 | 88 | 6 | 48 |
| B | 1 × 2 × 1 | 3 | 10 | 90 | 2 | 54 |
| C | 1 × 1 × 1 | 4 | 6 | 96 | 1 | 64 |
| D | 2 × 2 × 4 | $\frac{1}{2}$ | 40 | 10 | 16 | 2 |
| E | 4 × 2 × 4 | $\frac{3}{2}$ | 64 | 144 | 32 | 108 |

2. For each figure, A–E, the students should discover that the ratio of the corresponding surface areas of the image and the preimage is the square of the scale factor.

3. For each figure, A–E, the students should discover that the ratio of the corresponding volumes of the image and the preimage is the cube of the scale factor.

4. Students should state their conclusions clearly: the ratio of the surface area of each image to the surface area of its preimage is the square of the scale factor, and the ratio of the volume of each image to the volume of its preimage is the cube of the scale factor.

5. The volume of the scale model will be

$$100{,}000 \times \left(\frac{1}{100}\right)^3 = \frac{1}{10} \text{ ft}^3.$$

The students should recognize that they must multiply the volume of the building by the cube of the scale factor to find the volume of the model.

# Solutions for "Scale Models"

1. The scale factor is $\frac{1}{87}$. The students know that 1 foot equals 12 inches, so they can convert 7.25 feet to inches and then form a ratio:
$$\frac{1 \text{ inch}}{7.25 \text{ feet}} = \frac{1 \text{ inch}}{87 \text{ inches}} = \frac{1}{87}.$$

2. The scale factor is $\frac{1}{1,584,000}$. The students know that 1 mile equals 5,280 feet and 1 foot equals 12 inches, so they can convert 25 miles to 132,000 feet and to 1,584,000 inches. Then they can form a ratio:
$$\frac{1 \text{ inch}}{25 \text{ miles}} = \frac{1 \text{ inch}}{1,584,000 \text{ inches}} = \frac{1}{1,584,000}.$$

3. *a.* The scale factor is $\frac{1}{12}$. The students know that 1 foot equals 12 inches, so they can convert 6 feet to 72 inches and then form a ratio:
$$\frac{6 \text{ inches}}{6 \text{ feet}} = \frac{6 \text{ inches}}{72 \text{ inches}} = \frac{1}{12}.$$

   b. Students will suggest various dimensions. The area of the top of the Lilliputian's mattress is $\frac{1}{144}$, or $\left(\frac{1}{12}\right)^2$, times the area of the top of Gulliver's mattress. The students have previously discovered that the area of the image is the square of the scale factor times the area of the preimage.

   c. Students will suggest various dimensions. The volume of the Lilliputian's living room is $\frac{1}{1728}$, or $\left(\frac{1}{12}\right)^3$, times the volume of Gulliver's living room. The students have previously discovered that the volume of the image is the cube of the scale factor times the volume of the preimage.

4. Students' answers will vary, depending on their drawings and the scale factors that they select. The area of the image should be the product of the area of the preimage and the square of the scale factor.

# Solutions for "Fielding the Facts"

1. Fitness Field Day at Washington Elementary and Junior High School is dedicated to personal fitness. It is the concluding event in a monthlong celebration of fitness awareness. On this day, students complete in a number of outdoor athletic events.

2. Students might suggest that hosting Fitness Field Day at school would be convenient for a number of reasons: the school would have the necessary equipment for the events (for example, the high jump apparatus), the school has a responsibility to emphasize fitness to its students, and Fitness Field Day could build school spirit.

3. The track and field events are expected to be the central attraction at Fitness Field Day.

4. The organizers want the teams to be approximately equal in ability to ensure that they will be competitive; otherwise, the contests would not be fun. Teams with the most highly skilled athletes would win, and teams with less skilled athletes might lose motivation and enthusiasm.

5. Of the athletes whose results are displayed here, Michelle has the best time in the 800-meter race. Her time was the shortest: 2 minutes, 45 seconds. Students should recognize that a low score is desirable in this event.

6. Of the athletes whose results are displayed here, Judi was the weakest on the high jump. The height of her jump was the lowest: 3 feet, 6 inches. Students should recognize that a high score is best in this event.

## Solutions for "Fitness Fest Investigation"

Students' solutions will vary, and sample solutions from students are presented and discussed in the text (see pp. 59–61).

# References

Austin, Richard A., Denisse R. Thompson, and Charlene E. Beckmann. "Locusts for Lunch: Connecting Mathematics, Science, and Literature." *Mathematics Teaching in the Middle School* 12 (November 2006): 182–89.

Battista, Michael T. "The Development of a Cognition-Based Assessment System for Core Mathematics Concepts in Grades K–5." National Science Foundation Project, 2001.

Beckmann, Charlene E., Denisse R. Thompson, and Richard A. Austin. "Exploring Proportional Reasoning through Movies and Literature." *Mathematics Teaching in the Middle School* 9 (January 2004): 256–62.

Davidenko, Susana. "Building the Concept of Function from Students' Everyday Activities." *Mathematics Teacher* 90 (February 1997): 144–49.

Fennema, Elizabeth, Thomas P. Carpenter, Megan L. Franke, Linda Levi, Victoria R. Jacobs, and Susan B. Empson. "A Longitudinal Study of Learning to Use Children's Thinking in Mathematics Instruction." *Journal for Research in Mathematics Education* 27 (July 1996): 403–34.

Flores, Alfinio. "Hinged Geometry." *ON-Math* 4, no. 1 (2006).

Fraivillig, Judith. "Strategies for Advancing Children's Mathematical Thinking." *Teaching Children Mathematics* 7 (April 2001): 454–59.

Gregg, Diana Underwood. "Building Students' Sense of Linear Relationships by Stacking Cubes." *Mathematics Teacher* 95 (May 2002): 330–33.

Henningsen, Marjorie, and Mary Kay Stein. "Mathematical Tasks and Student Cognition: Classroom-Based Factors That Support and Inhibit High-Level Mathematical Thinking and Reasoning." *Journal for Research in Mathematics Education* 28 (November 1997): 524–49.

McCoy, Leah P. "Algebra: Real-Life Investigations in a Lab Setting." *Mathematics Teaching in the Middle School* 2 (February 1997): 220–24.

National Council of Teachers of Mathematics (NCTM). *Principles and Standards for School Mathematics.* Reston, Va.: NCTM, 2000.

———. *Curriculum Focal Points for Prekindergarten through Grade 8 Mathematics: A Quest for Coherence*, Reston, Va.: NCTM, 2006.

Pagni, David. "Finding Areas on Dot Paper." *Mathematics Teaching in the Middle School* 12 (December 2006/January 2007): 274–82.

Smith, Margaret Schwan, and Mary Kay Stein. "Selecting and Creating Mathematical Tasks: From Research to Practice." *Mathematics Teaching in the Middle School* 3 (February 1998): 344–50.

Stein, Mary Kay, Barbara W. Grover, and Marjorie Henningsen. "Building Student Capacity for Mathematical Thinking and Reasoning: An Analysis of Mathematical Tasks Used in Reform Classrooms." *American Educational Research Journal* 33 (1996): 455–88.

Stein, Mary Kay, and Margaret Schwan Smith. "Mathematical Tasks as a Framework for Reflection: From Research to Practice." *Mathematics Teaching in the Middle School* 3 (January 1998): 268–75.

Thompson, Denisse R., Michael Battista, Sally Mayberry, Karol L. Yeatts, and Judith S. Zawojewski. *Navigating through Problem Solving and Reasoning in*

*Grade 5. Principles and Standards for School Mathematics* Navigations Series. Reston, Va.: National Council of Teachers of Mathematics, 2007.

Willoughby, Stephen S. "Functions from Kindergarten through Sixth Grade." *Teaching Children Mathematics* 3 (February 1997): 314–18.

Yeatts, Karol L., Michael T. Battista, Sally Mayberry, Denisse R. Thompson, and Judith S. Zawojewski. *Navigating through Problem Solving and Reasoning in Grade 3. Principles and Standards for School Mathematics* Navigations Series. Reston, Va.: National Council of Teachers of Mathematics, 2004.

———. *Navigating through Problem Solving and Reasoning in Grade 4. Principles and Standards for School Mathematics* Navigations Series. Reston, Va.: National Council of Teachers of Mathematics, 2005.

## Suggested Reading

Crawford, Ann R., and William E. Scott. "Making Sense of Slope." *Mathematics Teacher* 93 (February 2000): 114–18.

Doerr, Helen M., and Lyn D. English. "A Modeling Perspective on Students' Mathematical Reasoning about Data." *Journal for Research in Mathematics Education* 34 (March 2003): 110–36.

Empson, Susan B. "Equal Sharing and the Roots of Fraction Equivalence." *Teaching Children Mathematics* 7 (March 2001): 421–25.

Fennema, Elizabeth, Thomas P. Carpenter, Megan L. Franke, Linda Levi, Victoria R. Jacobs, and Susan B. Empson. "A Longitudinal Study of Learning to Use Children's Thinking in Mathematics Instruction." *Journal for Research in Mathematics Education* 27 (July 1996): 403–34.

Flores, Alfinio, and Erika Klein. "From Students' Problem-Solving Strategies to Connections in Fractions." *Teaching Children Mathematics* 11 (May 2005): 452–57.

Kennedy, Leonard, and Steven Tipps. "Extending Understanding of Numbers and Numeration." In *Guiding Children's Learning of Mathematics*, edited by S. Branbant and E. Judd, pp. 229–64. Belmont, Calif.: Wadsworth Publishing Co., 1991.

Perlwitz, Marcela D. "Dividing Fractions: Reconciling Self-Generated Solutions with Algorithmic Answers." *Mathematics Teaching in the Middle School* 10 (February 2005): 278–83.

Piez, Cynthia M., and Mary H. Voxman. "Multiple Representations—Using Different Perspectives to Form a Clearer Picture." *Mathematics Teacher* 90 (February 1997): 164–66.

Smith, Margaret Schwan. "Redefining Success in Mathematics Teaching and Learning." *Mathematics Teaching in the Middle School* 5 (February 2000): 378–82, 86.

Wood, Terry, and Tammy Turner-Vorbeck. "Extending the Conception of Mathematics Teaching." In *Beyond Classical Pedagogy: Teaching Elementary School Mathematics*, edited by Terry Wood, Barbara Scott Nelson, and Janet Warfield, pp. 185–208. Mahwah, N.J.: Lawrence Erlbaum Associates, 2001.

Zawojewski, Judith S. "Polishing a Data Task: Seeking Better Assessment." *Teaching Children Mathematics* 2 (February 1996): 372–78.

Zawojewski, Judith S., Richard Lesh, and Lyn D. English. "A Models and

Modeling Perspective on the Role of Small Group Learning Activities." In *Beyond Constructivism: Models and Modeling Perspectives on Mathematics Problem Solving, Learning and Teaching*, edited by Richard Lesh and Helen M. Doerr, pp. 337–58. Mahwah, N.J.: Lawrence Erlbaum Associates, 2003.

# Children's Literature

Teachers may wish to incorporate appropriate literature into the investigations in this book. For children's books that are suitable for particular mathematics topics, teachers may refer to *The Wonderful World of Mathematics: A Critically Annotated List of Children's Books in Mathematics*, by Dianne Thiessen, Margaret Matthias, and Jacqueline Smith (Reston, Va.: NCTM, 1989). The examples of children's literature that are discussed in the text appear with annotations in the list below, along with other appropriate titles:

Adler, David A. *Fraction Fun*. New York: Holiday House, 1996.

Beneduce, Ann Keay. *Gulliver's Adventures in Lilliput*. New York: Putnam and Grosset, 1996.

>Gulliver is shipwrecked in Lilliput, where all the people are only six inches tall.

Briggs, Raymond. *Jim and the Beanstalk*. New York: Putnam and Grosset Group, 1997.

>Jim climbs a beanstalk and meets a giant who needs glasses, dentures, and a wig so he can see, eat, and look handsome. Jim uses a giant-sized coin to obtain each of the items the giant needs.

Burns, Marilyn. *The Greedy Triangle*. New York: Scholastic, Inc., 1994.

Dragonwagon, Crescent. *Half a Moon and One Whole Star*. New York: Macmillan, 1986.

Emberly, Ed. *Ed Emberly's Picture Pie: A Circle Drawing Book*. Boston: Little, Brown, 1984.

Gignti, Paul. *How Many Snails? A Counting Book*. New York: Greenwillow Books, 1988.

Hodges, Margaret. *Gulliver in Lilliput*. New York: Holiday House, 1995.

>Gulliver's travels in Lilliput are recounted in language for children. The illustrations help readers see the differences in the sizes of similar objects used by Gulliver and the Lilliputians.

Hutchins, Pat. *The Doorbell Rang*. New York: Greenwillow Books, 1986.

Lacapa, Kathleen, and Michael Lacapa. *Less than Half, More than Whole*. Flagstaff, Ariz.: Northland, 1994.

McCallum, Ann. *Beanstalk: The Measure of a Giant*. Watertown, Mass.: Charlesbridge Publishing, 2006.

>This take on the familiar tale about Jack and the beanstalk focuses on aspects of ratio as Jack compares himself to a giant boy named Ray.

McMillan, Bruce. *Eating Fractions*. New York: Scholastic Press, 1991.

Mathews, Louise. *Gator Pie*. New York: Dodd, Mead, 1979.

Murphy, Stuart J. *Give Me Half*. New York: HarperCollins Publishers, 1996.

Pallotta, Jerry. *The Hershey's Milk Chocolate Bar Fractions.* New York: Cartwheel Books, 1999.

Pomerantz, Charlotte. *The Half-Birthday Party.* New York: Clarion Books, 1984.

Schwartz, David M. *If Dogs Were Dinosaurs.* New York: Scholastic Press, 2005.

>The author makes humorous comparisons among many different objects, all involving aspects of scale.

———. *If You Hopped like a Frog.* New York: Scholastic Press, 1999.

>The author uses ideas of scale to make humorous comparisons with many objects.

Silverstein, Shel. "One Inch Tall." In *Where the Sidewalk Ends: The Poems and Drawings of Shel Silverstein*, p. 55. New York: Harper and Row, 1974.

>A one-inch-tall boy describes how he would accomplish several tasks, including wearing a thimble on his head as a hat.

Sundby, Scott. *Cut Down to Size at High Noon.* Watertown, Mass.: Charlesbridge Publishing, 2000.

>In the western town of Cowlick, a newcomer competes with the barber to scale objects of local significance up or down in elaborate hairstyles.

Suyeoko, George, Robert B. Goodman, and Robert A. Spicer. *Issunboshi.* Honolulu: Island Heritage Publishers, 1974.

>A one-inch boy protects a princess and wins her heart and hand. The story has an Asian cultural theme.

Watson, Clyde. *Tom Fox and the Apple Pie.* New York: Crowell, 1972.

Teachers may also wish to refer to the following books:

- *Exploring Mathematics through Literature: Articles and Lessons for Prekindergarten through Grade 8*, edited by Dianne Thiessen (NCTM 2004).

>This book provides classroom examples of the use of children's literature to teach problem solving, representation, and reasoning.

- *New Visions for Linking Literature and Mathematics*, by David J. Whitin and Phyllis Whitin (NCTM/National Council of Teachers of English 2004).

>This book helps teachers find and use age-appropriate books with mathematical content.